Start With Art

By BARBARA DONDIEGO
Illustrated by MARION HOPPING EKBERG & GARY MOHRMAN

DISCARD

Extend basic art activities with cross-curricular project books

Totline® Publications
A Division of Frank Schaffer Publications, Inc.
Torrance, California

Managing Editor: Kathleen Cubley
Editor: Marie Ianetti
Contributing Editors: Carol Gnojewski, Susan Hodges, Elizabeth McKinnon, Susan Sexton, Jean Warren
Copyeditor: Kris Fulsaas
Proofreader: Miriam Bulmer
Editorial Assistant: Durby Peterson
Graphic Designer (Interior): Sarah Ness
Graphic Designer (Cover): Brenda Mann Harrison
Illustrator (Cover): Kelly McMahon
Production Manager: Melody Olney

©1998 by Totline® Publications. All rights reserved. Except for the inclusion of brief quotations in a review, no part of this book may be reproduced or utilized in any form or by any means, electronic or mechanical, including photocopying, recording, or by any information storage and retrieval system, without written permission from the publisher.

ISBN: 1-57029-171-3

Library of Congress Catalog Card Number 98-60797
Printed in the United States of America
Published by Totline® Publications

Business Office: 23740 Hawthorne Blvd.
Torrance, CA 90505

Introduction

Start With Art provides your children with learning experiences to enjoy and remember. Inside, you will find instructions for 21 open-ended classroom art projects, each accompanied by a 6-page reproducible take-home book. By completing an art project and then making a book about the experience, your children express their creativity, expand their knowledge, and review important skills. And the resulting project books become treasured keepsakes to share with friends and family!

Start with Art introduces young artists to a variety of techniques, including drawing, painting, modeling, collage, and sculpting. Most of the art projects are simple enough to complete in a single day. Each project includes a materials list and complete instructions. As your children work, stand by to offer individual help as needed. When the art projects are complete, your children will be ready to construct their take-home books.

Each take-home book contains reproducible activity pages that review and build upon the art projects. These unique skill sheets are to be completed over a series of days, providing practice in representational drawing, writing, counting, sequencing, and more. Step-by-step instructions appear on the left-hand side of each reproducible page. Take note of any steps that may require special assistance. Photocopy the book pages and gather necessary supplies, such as writing and drawing materials, craft items, and glue. When the books are bound, these instructions will no longer be visible, and can be trimmed off if desired.

At home, parents will enjoy reading aloud the boldface text at the bottom of each page and talking with their child about the whole experience. Art is a wonderful way to draw a child into learning adventures, so *Start With Art,* and build basic skills, enhance literacy development, and send home a delightful souvenir!

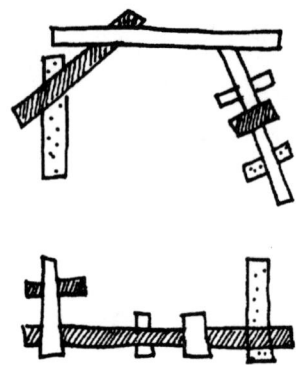

Contents

Activity Pages

Circle Art	9
Cookie Jars	10
Cotton Ball Chicks	11
Dough Letters	12
Dough Rainbows	13
Eggshell Art	14
Handy Puppets	15
Leis	16
Paint Mixing	17
Painted Paper Eggs	18
Paper Bag Puppets	19
Paper Cup Flowers	20
Paper Plate Hats	21
Paper Weaving	22
Rainy Day Pictures	23
Salt Pictures	24
Shape Lacing	25
Spatter-Painted Hearts	26
Tissue Paper Painting	27
Torn Paper Scenes	28
Wire Sculptures	29

Take-Home Books

My Circle Book	32
My Cookie Jar Book	38
My Cotton Ball Chick Book	44
My Dough Letter Book	50
My Rainbow Book	56
My Eggshell Art Book	62
My Handy Puppet Book	68
My Lei Book	74
My Paint Mixing Book	80
My Painted Paper Egg Book	86
My Paper Bag Puppet Book	92
My Paper Cup Flower Book	98
My Paper Plate Hat Book	104
My Paper Weaving Book	110
My Rainy Day Book	116
My Salt Picture Book	122
My Shape Lacing Book	128
My Heart Picture Book	134
My Tissue Paper Painting Book	140
My Torn Paper Book	146
My Wire Sculpture Book	152

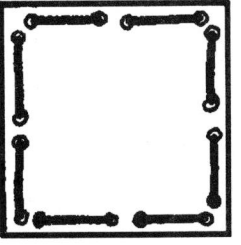
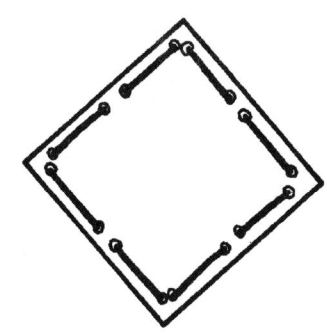
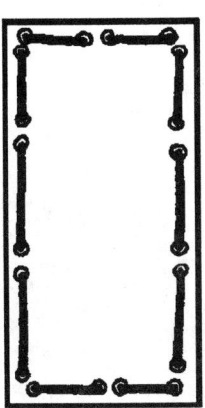
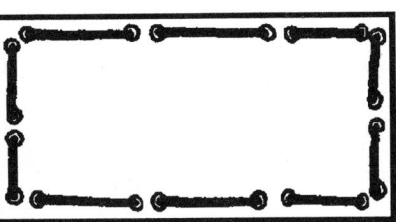
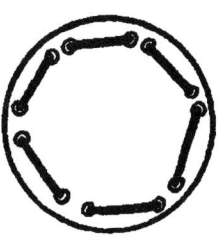

Activity Pages

Circle Art

You Will Need
- assorted paper (construction paper, gift-wrap, wrapping paper, etc.).
- child-safe scissors
- glue
- sheets of construction paper
- crayons

In advance, cut circles in a variety of sizes from assorted paper. Cut five or six circles for each of your children.

Invite the children to each choose several paper circles. Have them use scissors to cut some of their circles into halves and fourths. Let each child glue his or her cutouts onto construction paper to make a circle picture. Invite the children to use crayons to complete their pictures.

Making My Circle Book
1. Photocopy a set of pages 32–37 for each of your children.
2. Provide each child with a set of book pages. Read through the pages with your children, making sure they understand the activity directions on each page.
3. Have your children complete the activities while you provide help as needed.
4. Invite the children to decorate their book covers. They may wish to glue on buttons, O-shaped cereal pieces, reinforcement circles, or other round decorations.
5. Help your children arrange their book pages in order. Staple each book along the left hand edge.
6. Have your children "read" their books to you and to one another. Encourage them to take home their books and share them with their families.

Cookie Jars

You Will Need
- crayons or markers
- plain paper
- child-safe scissors
- glue
- construction paper
- small cookie cutters

In advance, draw a cookie jar outline on a sheet of plain paper, using the illustration on this page as a guide. Make a photocopy of this drawing for each of your children. Ask the children to cut out their cookie jar shapes and draw designs on them with crayons or markers. Have them glue only the top edge of the cookie jar shape to a sheet of construction paper. Show the children how to lift the flap to reveal the paper underneath. Then invite the children to each choose a few cookie cutters and trace around them on construction paper. Have them cut out the resulting cookie shapes. Let the children glue their cookie cutouts underneath their cookie jar shapes to make a lift-the-flap picture.

1.

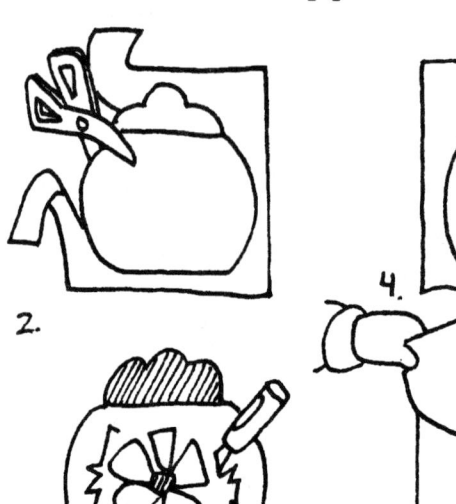
2.

3.

4.

5.

Making My Cookie Jar Book

1. Photocopy a set of pages 38–43 for each of your children.
2. Provide each child with a set of book pages. Read through the pages with your children, making sure they understand the activity directions on each page.
3. Have your children complete the activities while you provide help as needed.
4. Invite the children to decorate their book covers. They may wish to draw cookies.
5. Help your children arrange their book pages in order. Staple each book along the left hand edge.
6. Have your children "read" their books to you and to one another. Encourage them to take home their books and share them with their families.

Cotton Ball Chicks

You Will Need

- scissors
- orange construction paper
- egg cartons (1 egg cup per child)
- glue
- yellow cotton balls (2 per child)
- plastic googly eyes (2 per child)

In advance, cut orange construction paper into a small diamond shape for each of your children. Separate egg cartons into individual egg cups.

Have your children fold their diamond-shape papers to resemble a chick's beak. Then ask them to glue the two cotton balls together to resemble a chick's head and body. Let the children glue the googly eyes and beak onto the chick's head. Have them complete the project by gluing their cotton ball chick into an egg carton section.

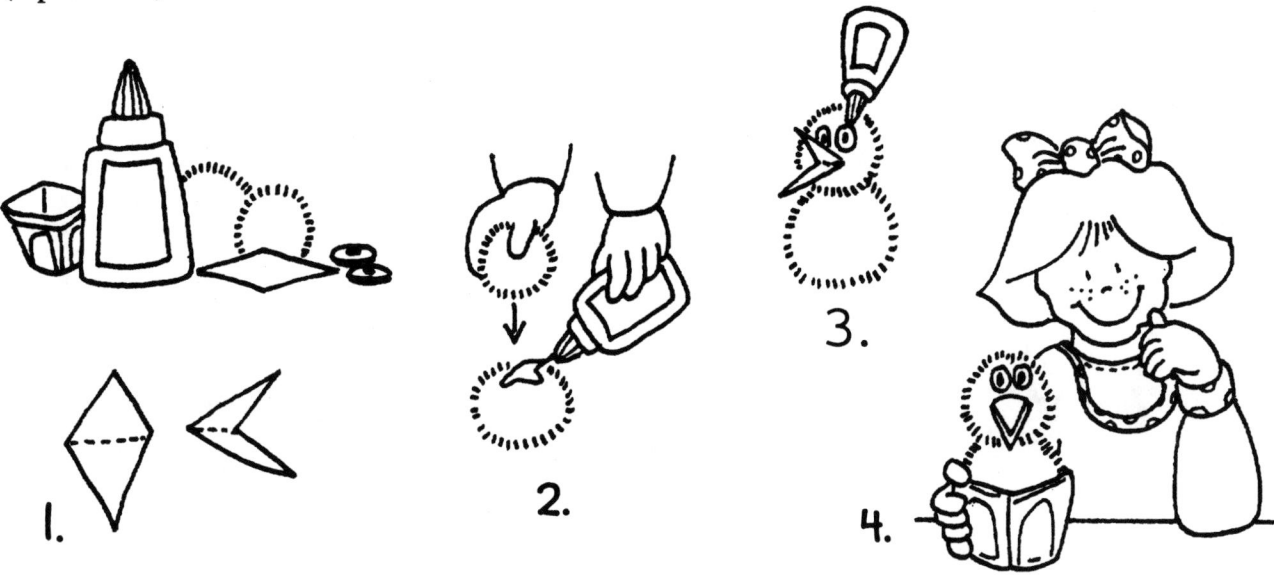

Making My Cotton Ball Chick Book

1. Photocopy a set of pages 44–49 for each of your children.
2. Provide each child with a set of book pages. Read through the pages with your children, making sure they understand the activity directions on each page.
3. Have your children complete the activities while you provide help as needed.
4. Invite the children to decorate their book covers. They may wish to use cotton balls or stickers.
5. Help your children arrange their book pages in order. Staple each book along the left hand edge.
6. Have your children "read" their books to you and to one another. Encourage them to take home their books and share them with their families.

Dough Letters

You Will Need

- modeling dough in assorted colors

Provide each of your children with a ball of modeling dough. Invite the children to roll their dough balls into short "stick" shapes and use these to form their favorite alphabet letters. (If necessary, review the formation of letters with your children, or have them look at a classroom letter chart for reference.) Let the children use pieces of dough in contrasting colors to decorate their creations.

Variation: To make durable dough letters, use salt dough instead of modeling dough. Bake the letters according to recipe instructions. Let your children paint their finished letters.

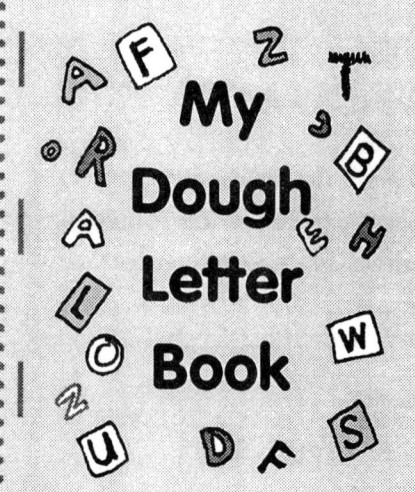

Making My Dough Letter Book

1. Photocopy a set of pages 50–55 for each of your children.
2. Provide each child with a set of book pages. Read through the pages with your children, making sure they understand the activity directions on each page.
3. Have your children complete the activities while you provide help as needed.
4. Invite the children to decorate their book covers. They may wish to write letters on the cover.
5. Help your children arrange their book pages in order. Staple each book along the left hand edge.
6. Have your children "read" their books to you and to one another. Encourage them to take home their books and share them with their families.

Dough Rainbows

You Will Need
- drawing or picture of a rainbow
- resealable plastic bags
- red, yellow, and blue modeling dough

Show your children a picture of a rainbow. Encourage them to notice the six major colors of the rainbow: red, orange, yellow, green, blue, and purple. Then provide each child with a resealable plastic bag containing modeling dough in the three primary colors (red, yellow, and blue). Challenge the children to make six little balls of dough in the colors of the rainbow. Help them discover how to combine the red, yellow, and blue dough to create the three secondary colors (orange, green, and purple). Then have the children roll their dough balls into "snakes" and arrange them to form a rainbow.

Making My Rainbow Book
1. Photocopy a set of pages 56–61 for each of your children.
2. Provide each child with a set of book pages. Read through the pages with your children, making sure they understand the activity directions on each page.
3. Have your children complete the activities, while you provide help as needed.
4. Invite the children to decorate their book covers. They may wish to draw rainbow designs with felt tip markers.
5. Help your children arrange their book pages in order. Staple each book along the left-hand edge.
6. Have your children "read" their books to you and to one another. Encourage them to take home their books and share them with their families.

Eggshell Art

You Will Need

- hard-cooked white eggs (1 per child)
- egg dye
- dipping containers
- resealable plastic bags
- index cards
- glue

In advance, prepare at least one hard-cooked white egg for each of your children. Mix red, yellow, green, and blue egg dye, and pour the dye into dipping containers.

Invite each of your children to dye a hard-cooked egg in the color of his or her choice. Allow the eggs to dry. Then serve each child his or her dyed egg in a resealable plastic bag. Let the children eat their egg and ask them to put their eggshells in their plastic bag. Help the children seal their bag, then let them crush the shells within.

Provide each child with an index card. Invite the children to make collages by gluing their colored eggshells to their index card.

Making My Eggshell Art Book

1. Photocopy a set of pages 62–67 for each of your children.
2. Provide each child with a set of book pages. Read through the pages with your children, making sure they understand the activity directions on each page.
3. Have your children complete the activities while you provide help as needed.
4. Invite the children to decorate their book covers. They may wish to glue colored rice to the covers, or draw with felt tip markers.
5. Help your children arrange their book pages in order. Staple each book along the left hand edge.
6. Have your children "read" their books to you and to one another. Encourage them to take home their books and share them with their families.

Handy Puppets

You Will Need
- construction paper
- crayons
- child-safe scissors
- glue
- decorative items
- craft sticks

Give each of your children a piece of construction paper. Have each child place one hand on the paper. Help the children trace around their hand with a crayon. Let the children cut out their hand-shape outlines. (Cutting will be easier if the outlines are not too detailed.) Invite the children to glue decorative items such as googly eyes, feathers, or felt scraps to their hand cutouts. Allow the glue to dry. Have the children glue their decorated hand shapes to craft sticks to make stick puppets.

Making My Handy Puppet Book

1. Photocopy a set of pages 68–73 for each of your children.
2. Provide each child with a set of book pages. Read through the pages with your children, making sure they understand the activity directions on each page.
3. Have your children complete the activities while you provide help as needed.
4. Invite the children to decorate their book covers. They may wish to draw a hand border or attach handprint stickers to the cover.
5. Help your children arrange their book pages in order. Staple each book along the left hand edge.
6. Have your children "read" their books to you and to one another. Encourage them to take home their books and share them with their families.

15

Leis

You Will Need
- tissue paper
- yarn
- tape
- child-safe scissors
- drinking straws

Precut a generous supply of 3-inch circles, squares, and triangles out of tissue paper. Punch a hole in the center of each shape. Give each of your children a piece of yarn about 2 feet long. Have the children tie a knot in one end of the yarn and wrap tape around the other end to make a "needle." Provide the children with drinking straws and scissors, and let them snip the straws into pieces. Then have them string the straw pieces and paper flowers on their yarn to make "leis." As the children finish, tie their leis around their necks.

Making My Lei Book

1. Photocopy a set of pages 74–79 for each of your children.
2. Provide each child with a set of book pages. Read through the pages with your children, making sure they understand the activity directions on each page.
3. Have your children complete the activities while you provide help as needed.
4. Invite the children to decorate their book covers. They may wish to draw flowers.
5. Help your children arrange their book pages in order. Staple each book along the left hand edge.
6. Have your children "read" their books to you and to one another. Encourage them to take home their books and share them with their families.

Paint Mixing

You Will Need

- divided plates (infant plates work well)
- tempera paint in several colors
- smocks
- paintbrushes
- large sheets of art paper

In advance, prepare a paint palette for each of your children by pouring a different color of tempera paint into two small sections of a divided plate. Leave the large section empty.

Invite your children to put on a smock and make a painting. Encourage the children to mix and swirl the two colors of paint with a paintbrush, creating a third color of paint on the palette. Have them use the paint on their palette to make a painting on a large sheet of paper. Let the children repeat the activity, if you wish, using clean sheets of paper and new palettes with two different colors of paint.

Making My Paint Mixing Book

1. Photocopy a set of pages 80–85 for each of your children.
2. Provide each child with a set of book pages. Read through the pages with your children, making sure they understand the activity directions on each page.
3. Have your children complete the activities while you provide help as needed.
4. Invite the children to decorate their book covers. They may wish to add paint splotches or other colorful touches.
5. Help your children arrange their book pages in order. Staple each book along the left hand edge.
6. Have your children "read" their books to you and to one another. Encourage them to take home their books and share them with their families.

Painted Paper Eggs

You Will Need

- scissors
- construction paper
- evaporated milk
- shallow plastic containers
- food coloring
- paintbrushes

Ahead of time, cut a few egg shapes from construction paper for each of your children. Pour evaporated milk into shallow plastic containers. Use food coloring to tint the milk in the containers. Invite your children to paint designs on the egg cutouts with the tinted milk.

Making My Painted Paper Egg Book

1. Photocopy a set of pages 86–91 for each of your children.
2. Provide each child with a set of book pages. Read through the pages with your children, making sure they understand the activity directions on each page.
3. Have your children complete the activities while you provide help as needed.
4. Invite the children to decorate their book covers. They may wish to use egg stickers or small egg cutouts.
5. Help your children arrange their book pages in order. Staple each book along the left hand edge.
6. Have your children "read" their books to you and to one another. Encourage them to take home their books and share them with their families.

Paper Bag Puppets

You Will Need
- paper lunch bags
- markers
- child-safe scissors
- construction paper scraps
- decorative items
- glue

Provide each of your children with a paper lunch bag. Set out markers, scissors, construction paper scraps, and decorative items such as ribbon, yarn, foil, and cotton balls. Invite your children to use these materials to turn their paper bags into hand puppets. Encourage each child to think of a character he or she would like to make. Then have the children lay their bag on the table either vertically or horizontally and glue on the materials to make the puppet of their choice.

Making My Paper Bag Puppet Book
1. Photocopy a set of pages 92–97 for each of your children.
2. Provide each child with a set of book pages. Read through the pages with your children, making sure they understand the activity directions on each page.
3. Have your children complete the activities while you provide help as needed.
4. Invite the children to decorate their book covers. They may wish to use torn pieces of a paper bag.
5. Help your children arrange their book pages in order. Staple each book along the left hand edge.
6. Have your children "read" their books to you and to one another. Encourage them to take home their books and share them with their families.

Paper Cup Flowers

You Will Need

- crayons
- small paper cups (2 or 3 per child)
- child-safe scissors
- pencil
- chenille stems (2 or 3 per child)
- large paper cups (1 per child)
- modeling clay

Invite your children to use crayons to decorate the inside and outside surfaces of small paper cups. Demonstrate how to cut a cup into a flower shape, using scissors to make five or six cuts down the cup to about 1 inch from the bottom, then curling the edges of the cut strips over a pencil and away from the center to form "petals." Let each child make two or three flowers in this fashion, while you offer help as needed. To complete each flower, poke the end of a chenille stem up through the bottom of the cup and twist it into a knot, forming a flower stem below. Have each child arrange the paper cup flowers in a larger plastic cup half-filled with modeling clay.

Making My Paper Cup Flower Book

1. Photocopy a set of pages 98–103 for each of your children.
2. Provide each child with a set of book pages. Read through the pages with your children, making sure they understand the activity directions on each page.
3. Have your children complete the activities while you provide help as needed.
4. Invite the children to decorate their book covers. They may wish to draw flowers with crayons or markers, or add flower stickers to the cover.
5. Help your children arrange their book pages in order. Staple each book along the left hand edge.
6. Have your children "read" their books to you and to one another. Encourage them to take home their books and share them with their families.

Paper Plate Hats

You Will Need
- paper plates
- child-safe scissors
- decorative items
- glue

Provide each of your children with a paper plate. Demonstrate how to fold the plate in half and then cut a semicircle along the folded edge to make a hat with an open crown. Have the children cut their plates into hats. Set out decorative items such as yarn, markers, glue, doilies, stickers, paper scraps, and pompons. Encourage your children to use these materials to decorate their hats. They may wish to glue yarn "hair" to the brim of their hat, cut up the center section of the plate and glue it to the brim, or add flower stickers and lacy doilies to make a frilly bonnet.

Making My Paper Plate Hat Book

1. Photocopy a set of pages 104–109 for each of your children.
2. Provide each child with a set of book pages. Read through the pages with your children, making sure they understand the activity directions on each page.
3. Have your children complete the activities while you provide help as needed.
4. Invite the children to decorate their book covers. They may wish to glue on art materials.
5. Help your children arrange their book pages in order. Staple each book along the left hand edge.
6. Have your children "read" their books to you and to one another. Encourage them to take home their books and share them with their families.

Paper Weaving

You Will Need

- 12-by-18-inch construction paper
- pencil
- ruler
- child-safe scissors
- transparent tape
- stickers (optional)

In advance, prepare a paper loom and paper strips for each of your children. To make a paper loom, fold a 12-by-18-inch piece of construction paper in half, so that the short ends touch. With a pencil, draw lines about 1 inch apart, starting at the folded edge and stopping 2 inches short of the open edge. To make paper strips, cut construction paper into 12-by-1-inch pieces. (Each child will need about a dozen strips.)

Invite your children to each choose a loom and a supply of strips. Ask the children to cut along the pencil lines on the folded paper. Then have them open their papers to reveal a series of slats. Demonstrate how to weave the paper strips through the slats, pushing the paper over one slat and under the next. Let the children weave their paper strips into their looms to make a woven mat. As the children finish their mats, have them tape the ends of the strips to the loom. If you wish, have the children decorate their finished mats with stickers.

Making My Paper Weaving Book

1. Photocopy a set of pages 110–115 for each of your children.
2. Provide each child with a set of book pages. Read through the pages with your children, making sure they understand the activity directions on each page.
3. Have your children complete the activities while you provide help as needed.
4. Invite the children to decorate their book covers. They may wish to glue on paper strips or other decorations.
5. Help your children arrange their book pages in order. Staple each book along the left hand edge.
6. Have your children "read" their books to you and to one another. Encourage them to take home their books and share them with their families.

Rainy Day Pictures

You Will Need
- white construction paper
- markers
- hole punches
- light blue construction paper
- glue

Provide each of your children with a sheet of white construction paper. Have the children use markers to draw an outdoor scene on their papers. Then give each child a hole punch and a half sheet of light blue construction paper. Have the children punch holes from the light blue construction paper and glue the resulting "raindrops" to their outdoor scenes.

Variation: Have the children glue their "raindrops" to magazine pictures instead of drawings.

Making My Rainy Day Book
1. Photocopy a set of pages 116–121 for each of your children.
2. Provide each child with a set of book pages. Read through the pages with your children, making sure they understand the activity directions on each page.
3. Have your children complete the activities while you provide help as needed.
4. Invite the children to decorate their book covers. They may wish to draw raindrops or umbrellas.
5. Help your children arrange their book pages in order. Staple each book along the left hand edge.
6. Have your children "read" their books to you and to one another. Encourage them to take home their books and share them with their families.

Salt Pictures

You Will Need
- white construction paper
- crayons
- paintbrushes
- shallow containers
- glue
- table salt in shakers

Provide your children with white construction paper and crayons. Invite them to draw pictures with these supplies. Then set out paintbrushes, shallow containers of glue, and shakers of table salt. Have the children brush glue on their drawings and then sprinkle salt on top of the wet glue. Help them shake off the excess salt and allow the pictures to dry. When the glue dries, the salt will leave a shimmering residue.

Making My Salt Picture Book
1. Photocopy a set of pages 122–127 for each of your children.
2. Provide each child with a set of book pages. Read through the pages with your children, making sure they understand the activity directions on each page.
3. Have your children complete the activities, while you provide help as needed.
4. Invite the children to decorate their book covers. They may wish to glue salt on the cover.
5. Help your children arrange their book pages in order. Staple each book along the left-hand edge.
6. Have your children "read" their books to you and to one another. Encourage them to take home their books and share them with their families.

Shape Lacing

You Will Need
- plastic-foam food trays
- pencils
- child-safe scissors
- hole punch
- shoelaces

Provide each of your children with a plastic-foam food tray, a pencil, and scissors. (Unused food trays are available from grocery stores for a nominal price.) Have the children draw shapes on their food trays. Then let them use scissors to cut out the shapes. For each child, use a hole punch to make lacing holes around the outside edge of the plastic-foam shape. Then give each child a shoelace knotted at one end. Invite the children to thread their shoelaces around their shapes.

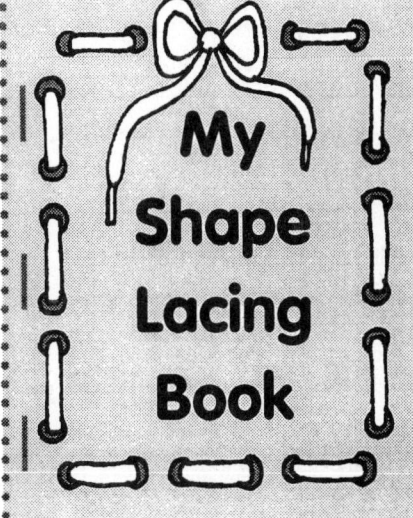

Making My Shape Lacing Book
1. Photocopy a set of pages 128–133 for each of your children.
2. Provide each child with a set of book pages. Read through the pages with your children, making sure they understand the activity directions on each page.
3. Have your children complete the activities, while you provide help as needed.
4. Invite the children to decorate their book covers. They may wish to punch holes around the cover with a hole punch and then thread a piece of yarn through the holes.
5. Help your children arrange their book pages in order. Staple each book along the left-hand edge.
6. Have your children "read" their books to you and to one another. Encourage them to take home their books and share them with their families.

Spatter-Painted Hearts

You Will Need

- scissors
- construction paper
- ruler
- newspaper
- mesh strainers
- clean plastic food containers (about 3 per table)
- water
- food coloring
- black felt tip pens
- old toothbrushes (sanitized in a bleach solution)
- glue

In advance, cut 2-, 3-, and 4-inch heart shapes from several colors of construction paper. (Cut three or four hearts for each of your children.) Cover the tables in your art area with newspaper. At each table, set out white construction paper, two or more mesh strainers, and a few plastic food containers filled with tinted water.

Invite your children to each choose three or four heart cutouts and write their names on the back of the shapes. Have the children arrange their heart shapes on the newspaper. Show the children how to invert a strainer over a heart cutout, dip a toothbrush into tinted water, and rub the toothbrush over the strainer to create a spatter-paint effect. Let the children spatter-paint their heart shapes, using as many colors of water as desired. Allow the painted shapes to dry. The next day, have the children glue their heart cutouts to a large sheet of white construction paper to make animals or other designs.

Making My Heart Picture Book

1. Photocopy a set of pages 134–139 for each of your children.
2. Provide each child with a set of book pages. Read through the pages with your children, making sure they understand the activity directions on each page.
3. Have your children complete the activities, while you provide help as needed.
4. Invite the children to decorate their book covers. They may wish to glue on heart shapes.
5. Help your children arrange their book pages in order. Staple each book along the left-hand edge.
6. Have your children "read" their books to you and to one another. Encourage them to take home their books and share them with their families.

Tissue Paper Painting

You Will Need
- tissue paper
- construction paper
- small container
- water

Provide each of your children with a few 6-inch tissue paper squares in assorted colors, a sheet of construction paper, and a small container of water. Have the children scrunch their tissue paper squares, dip them in water, and smear them on the construction paper to make a painting. Encourage the children to hold more than one piece of tissue paper at a time to mix the colors. Lay the papers flat to dry.

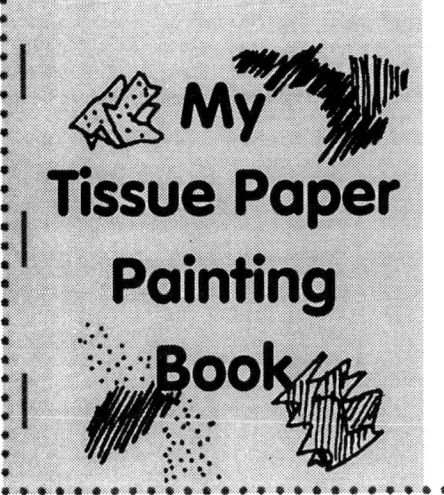

Making My Tissue Paper Painting Book

1. Photocopy a set of pages 140–145 for each of your children.
2. Provide each child with a set of book pages. Read through the pages with your children, making sure they understand the activity directions on each page.
3. Have your children complete the activities, while you provide help as needed.
4. Invite the children to decorate their book covers. They may wish to glue on pieces of tissue paper.
5. Help your children arrange their book pages in order. Staple each book along the left-hand edge.
6. Have your children "read" their books to you and to one another. Encourage them to take home their books and share them with their families.

Torn Paper Scenes

You Will Need
- white construction paper
- construction paper scraps
- glue

Provide each of your children with a sheet of white construction paper and several construction paper scraps in various colors. Have the children tear the scraps into smaller pieces or shapes. Ask the children to glue the torn paper to the white construction paper to make a collage or other scene.

Making My Torn Paper Book
1. Photocopy a set of pages 146–151 for each of your children.
2. Provide each child with a set of book pages. Read through the pages with your children, making sure they understand the activity directions on each page.
3. Have your children complete the activities while you provide help as needed.
4. Invite the children to decorate their book covers. They may with to glue on torn pieces of construction paper.
5. Help your children arrange their book pages in order. Staple each book along the left hand edge.
6. Have your children "read" their books to you and to one another. Encourage them to take home their books and share them with their families.

Wire Sculptures

You Will Need
- plastic-foam food trays
- chenille stems
- scissors
- ballpoint pens
- tape

Provide each of your children with a clean plastic-foam food tray (available for a nominal cost from your local grocery store), several chenille stems cut in various sizes, and a ballpoint pen. Invite the children to use these materials to make sculptures. Have them begin by using the pen to poke a small hole in the food tray. Then have them insert one end of a chenille stem into this hole. Show them how to secure the stem to the tray by bending the end of the stem and taping it to the bottom of the tray. (Be ready to assist your children with this step.) Demonstrate how to bend the stem into a shape. Let your children continue in this manner, attaching more stems to their bases and bending them to make wire sculptures.

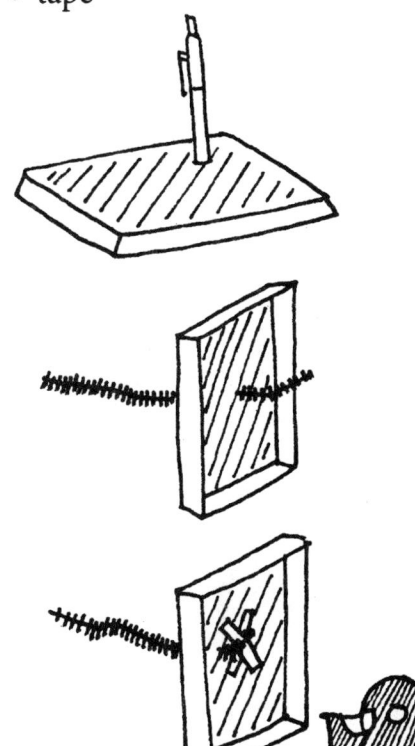

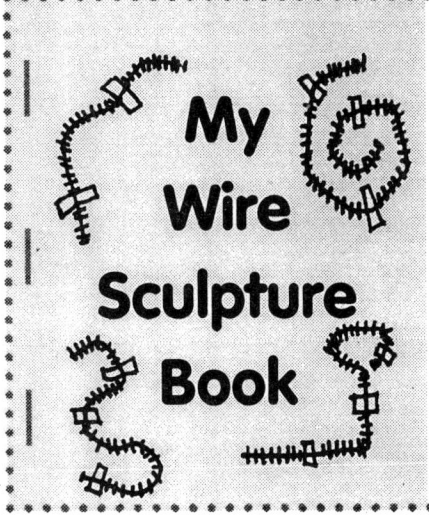

Making My Wire Sculpture Book
1. Photocopy a set of pages 152–157 for each of your children.
2. Provide each child with a set of book pages. Read through the pages with your children, making sure they understand the activity directions on each page.
3. Have your children complete the activities, while you provide help as needed.
4. Invite the children to decorate their book covers. They may wish to use chenille stems or other materials.
5. Help your children arrange their book pages in order. Staple each book along the left-hand edge.
6. Have your children "read" their books to you and to one another. Encourage them to take home their books and share them with their families.

Take Home Books

My Circle Book

By _____

1. Draw your circle art.
2. Color your picture.

My circle picture looked like this.

1. Read the rhyme.
2. Count the circles.
3. Fill in the blank.

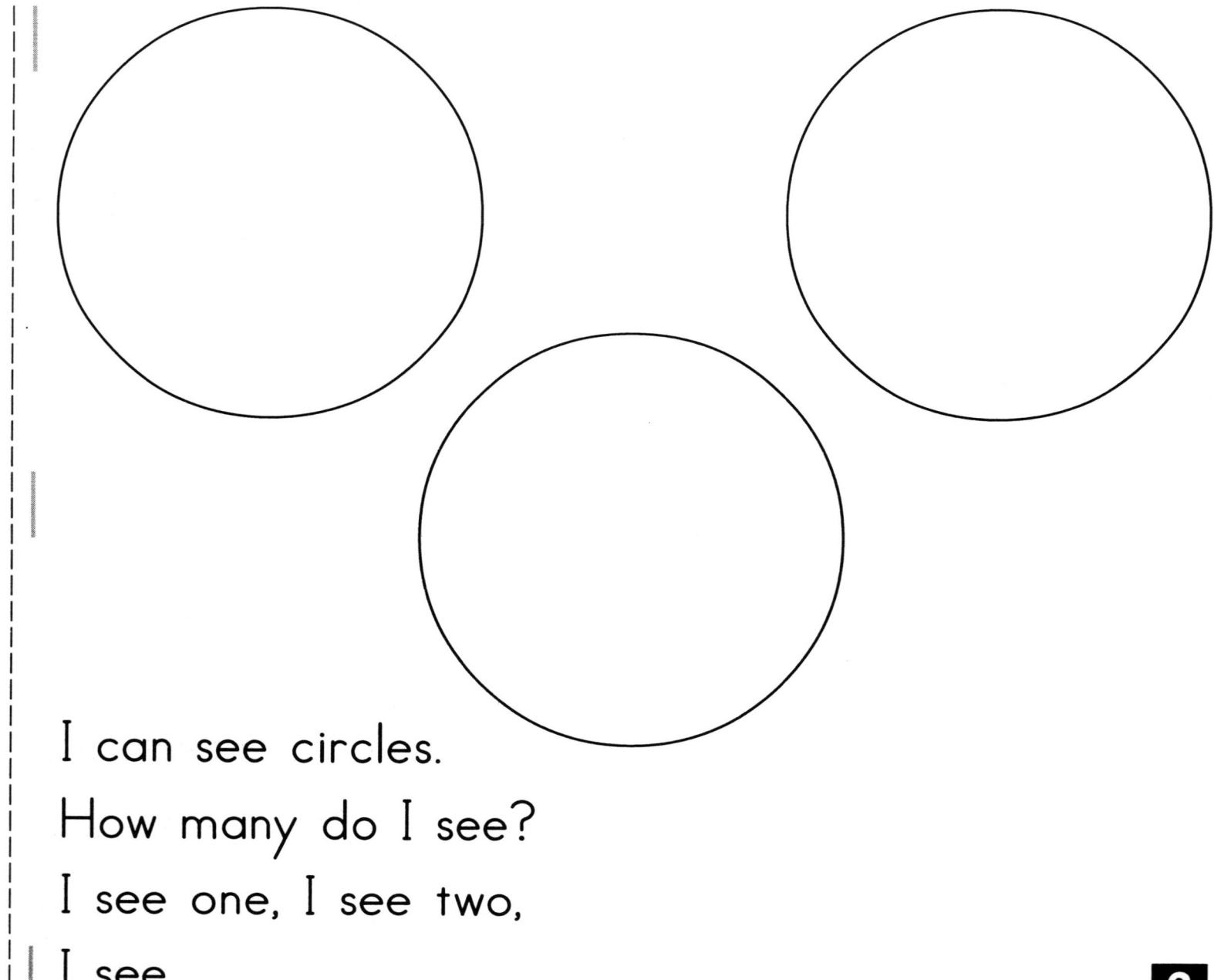

I can see circles.
How many do I see?
I see one, I see two,
I see _____.

1. Count the balloons.
2. Write the number.

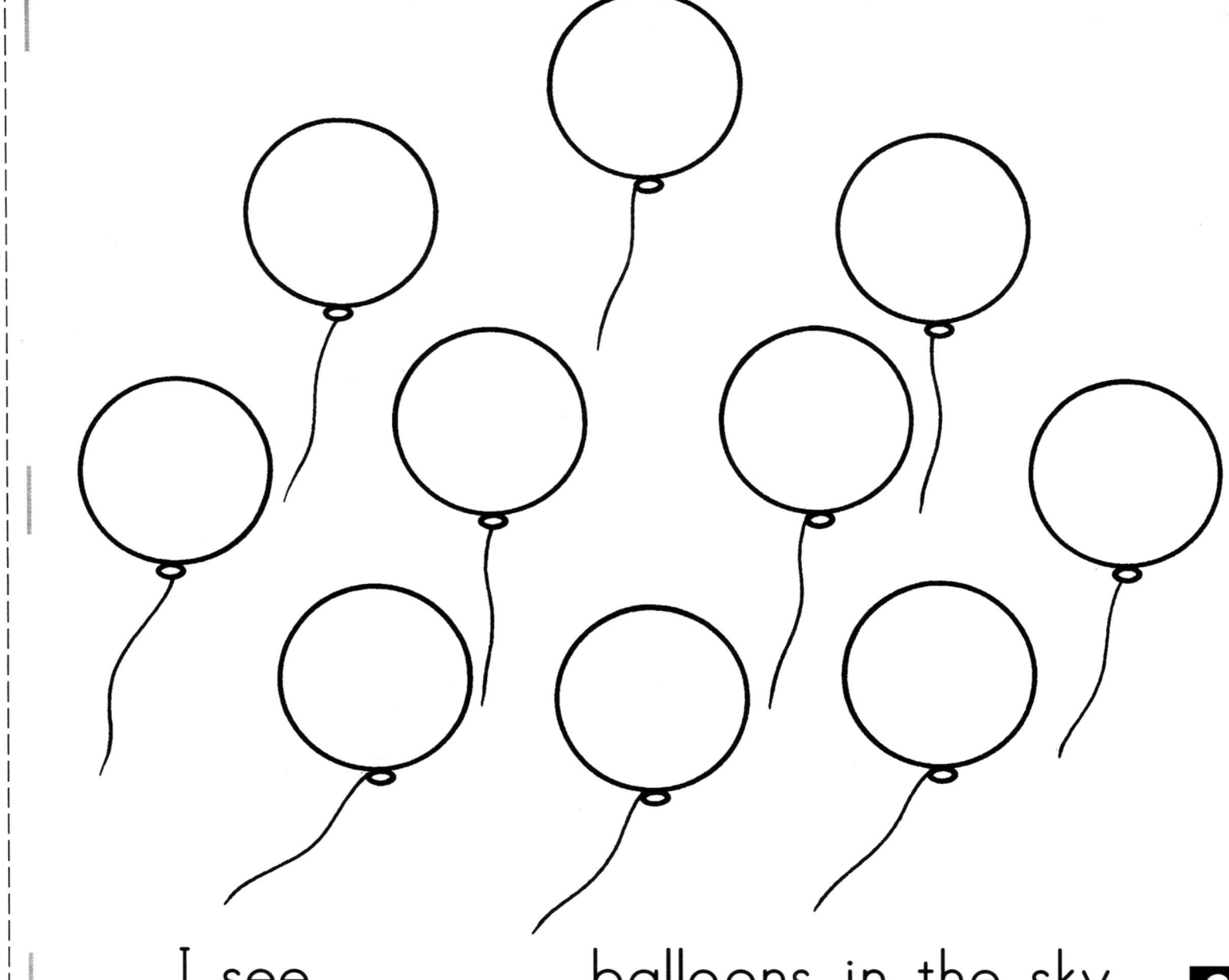

I see _____ balloons in the sky.

1. Draw a picture of something round.
2. Fill in the blank.

The _____ is round like a circle.

1. Count the parts.
2. Write the number.
3. Color the circles.

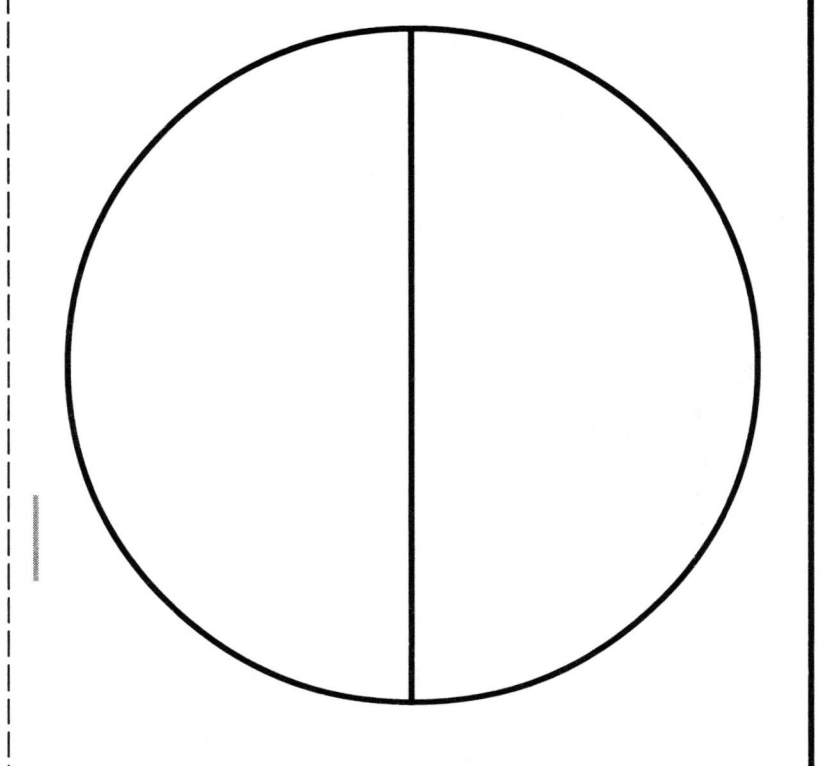

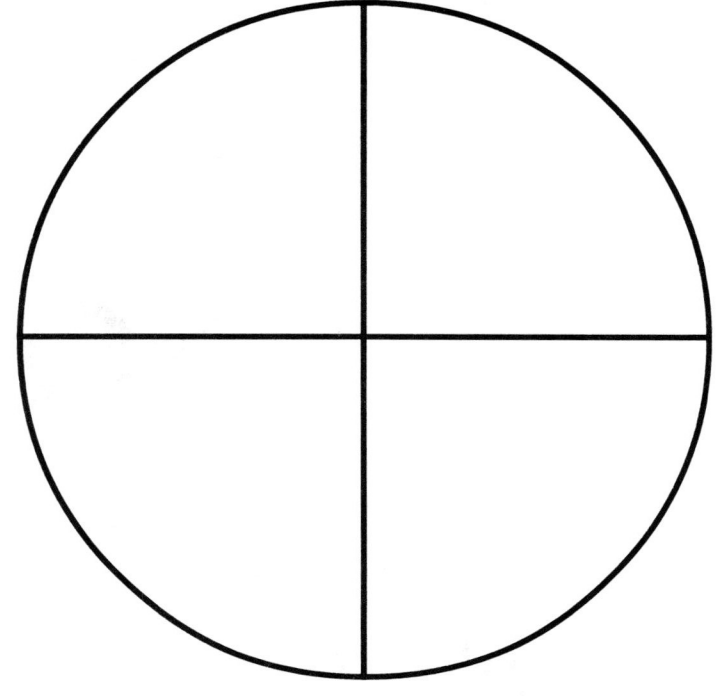

This circle is cut into _____ parts.

This circle is cut into _____ parts.

My Cookie Jar Book

By _____

© 1998 Totline® Publications
(reproducible) p38

1. Draw a picture of your cookie jar.

My cookie jar looked like this.

© 1998 Totline® Publications
(reproducible) p39

1

1. Draw your favorite cookie on the plate.

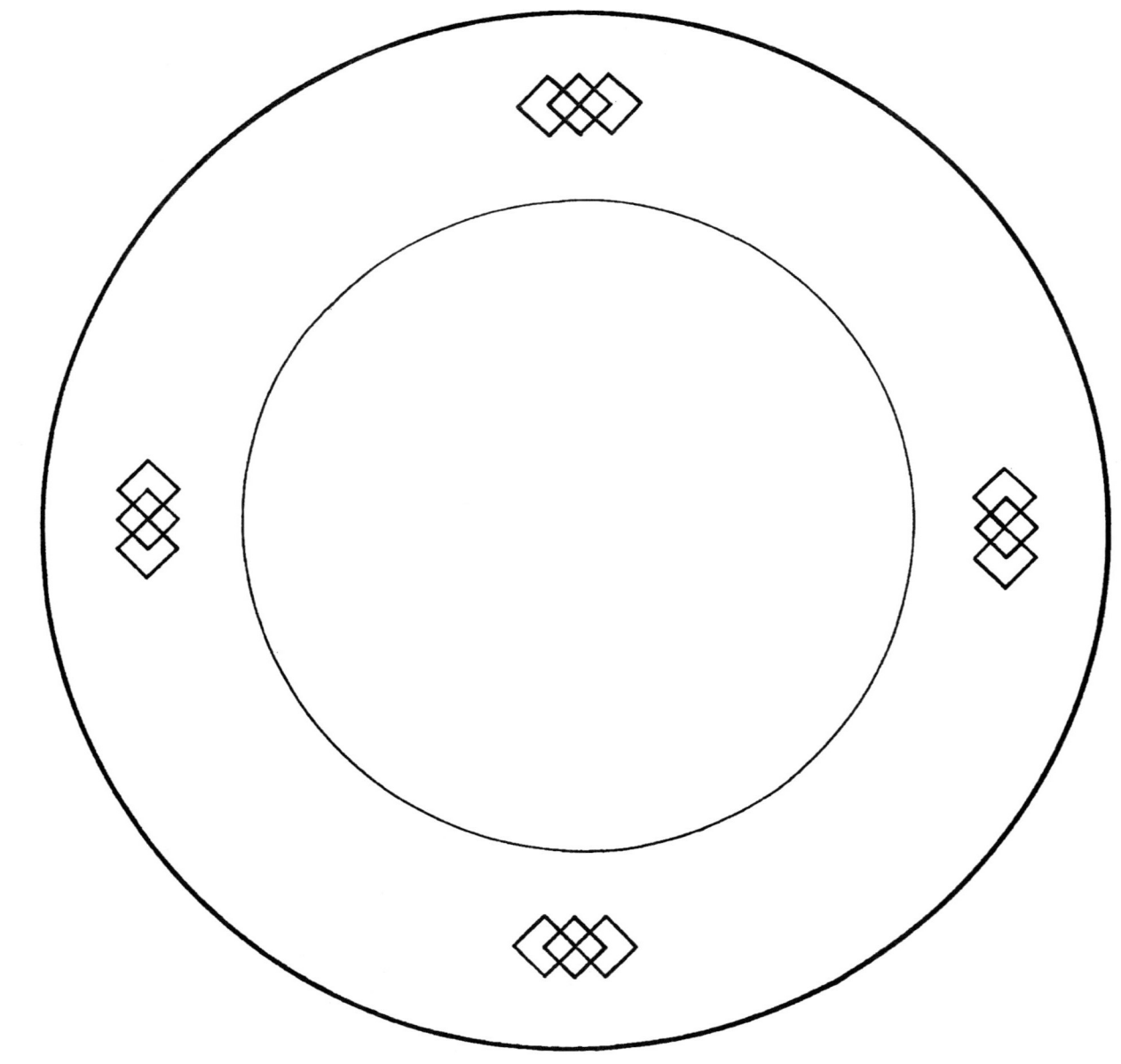

My favorite cookie looked like this.

1. Color the matching cookies the same color.

Some cookies match.

1. Read the numeral.
2. Draw chips on each cookie to match the number.

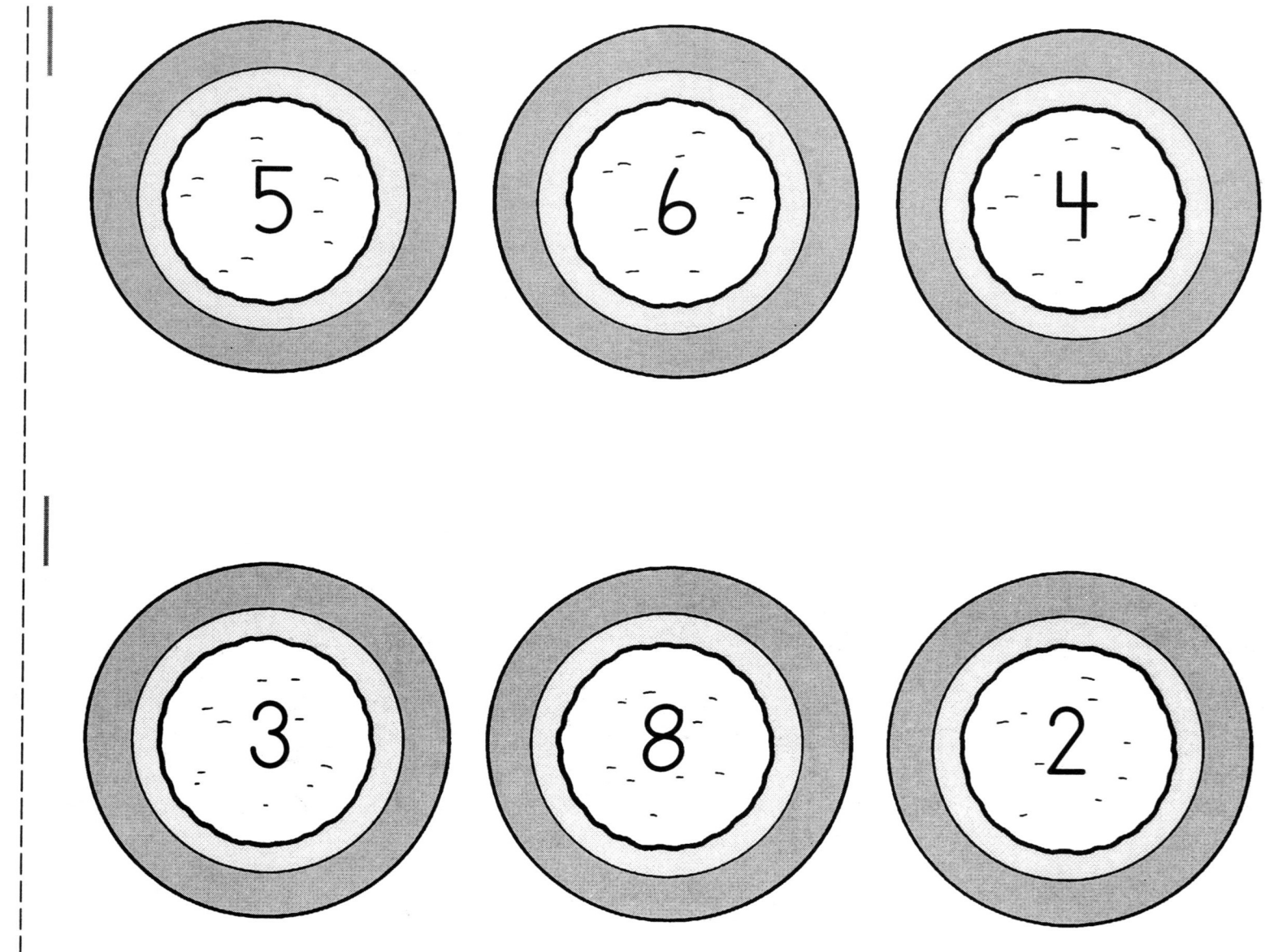

These cookies have lots of chips.

1. Start at the *.
2. Connect the dots.
3. Draw cookies in the jar.

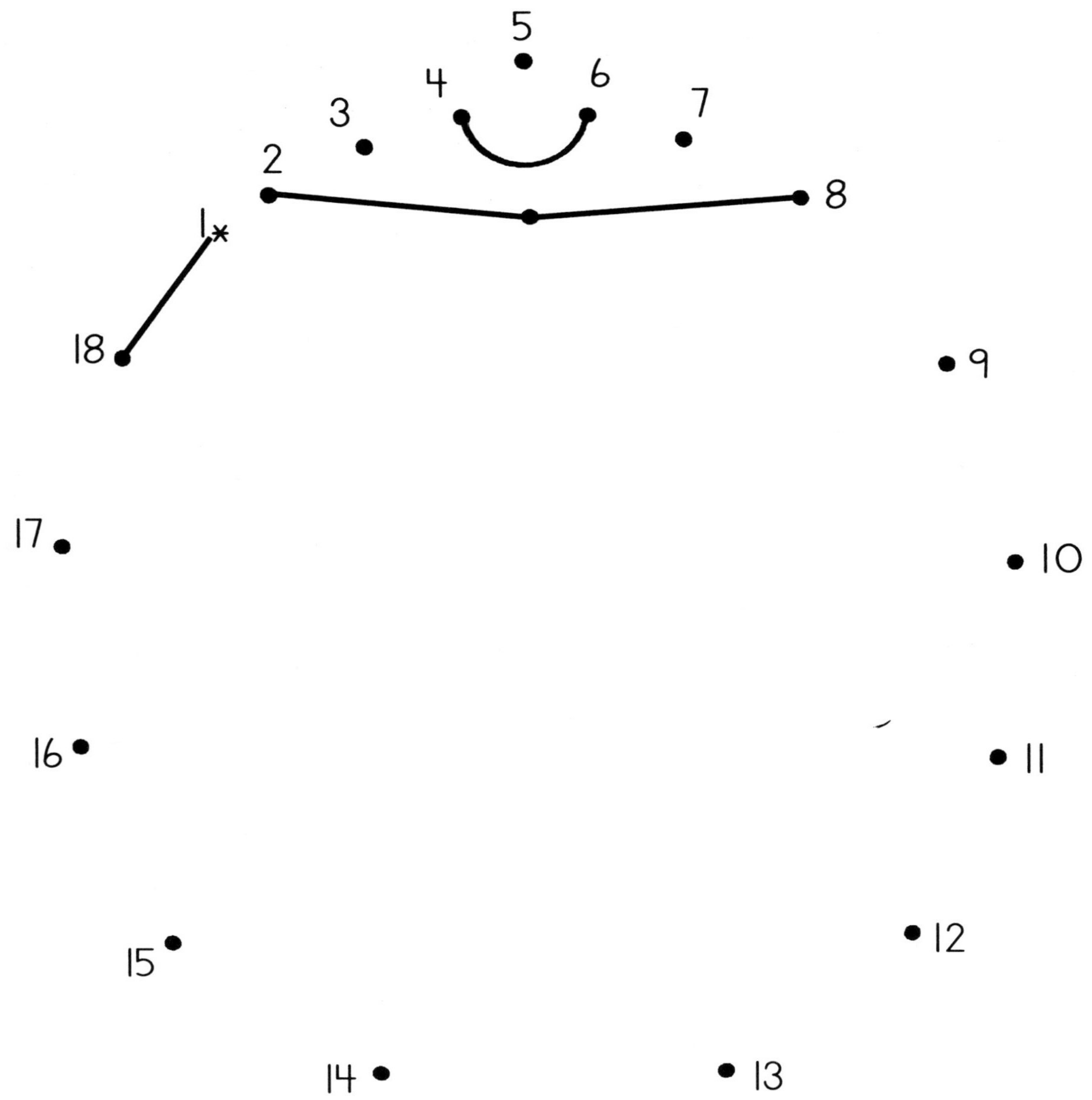

I see a cookie jar.

My Cotton Ball Chick Book

By _____

© 1998 Totline® Publications
(reproducible) p44

1. Draw a picture of your chick.
2. Color the picture.

My chick looked like this.

1. Circle the things that are soft.

These things are soft like cotton balls.

1. Help the chick find its mother.

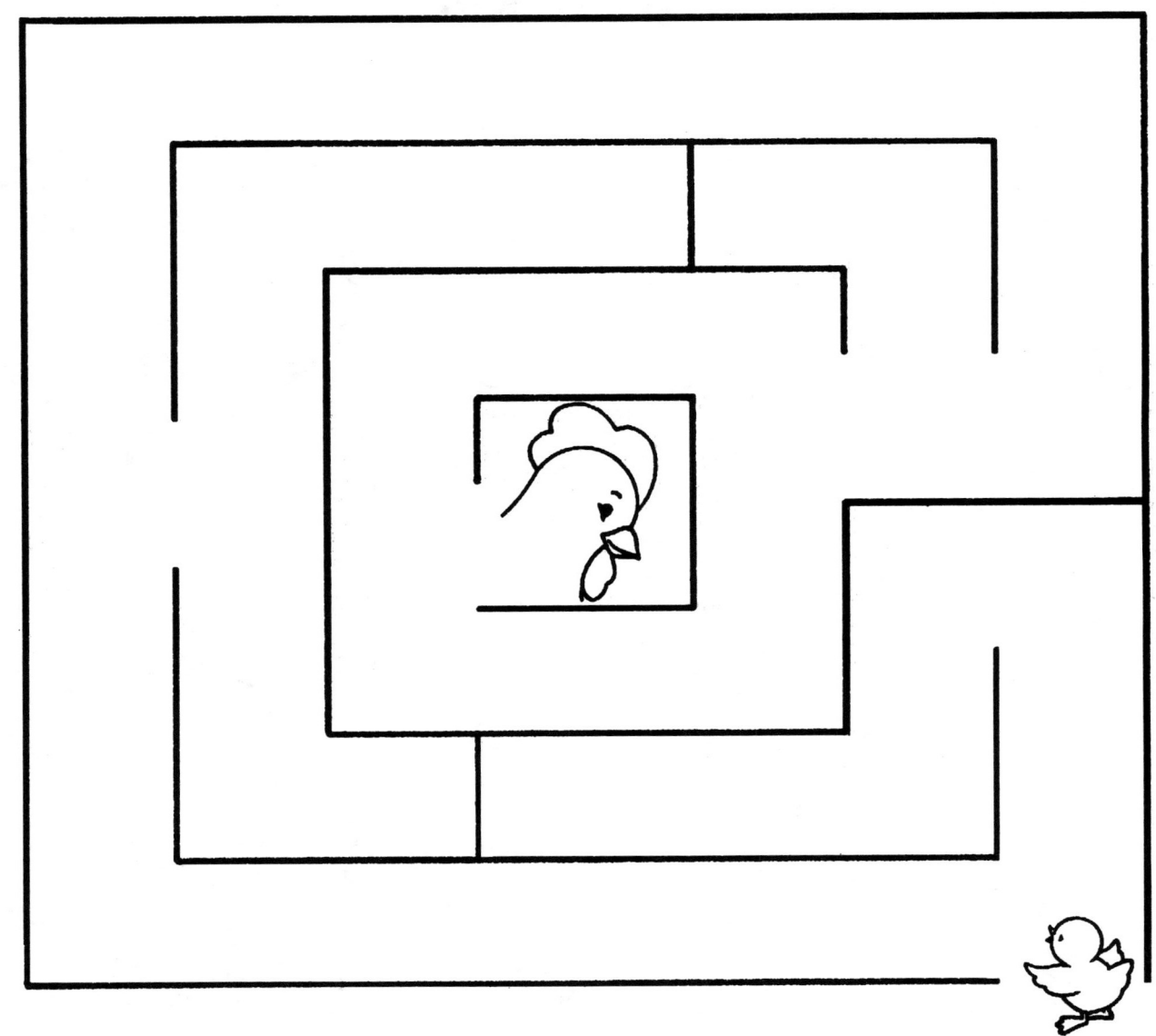

The chick found its mother.

1. Read the numeral.
2. Draw eggs in the nest to match the number.

I put eggs in the nests.

1. Begin at the *.
2. Connect the dots.
3. Color the picture.

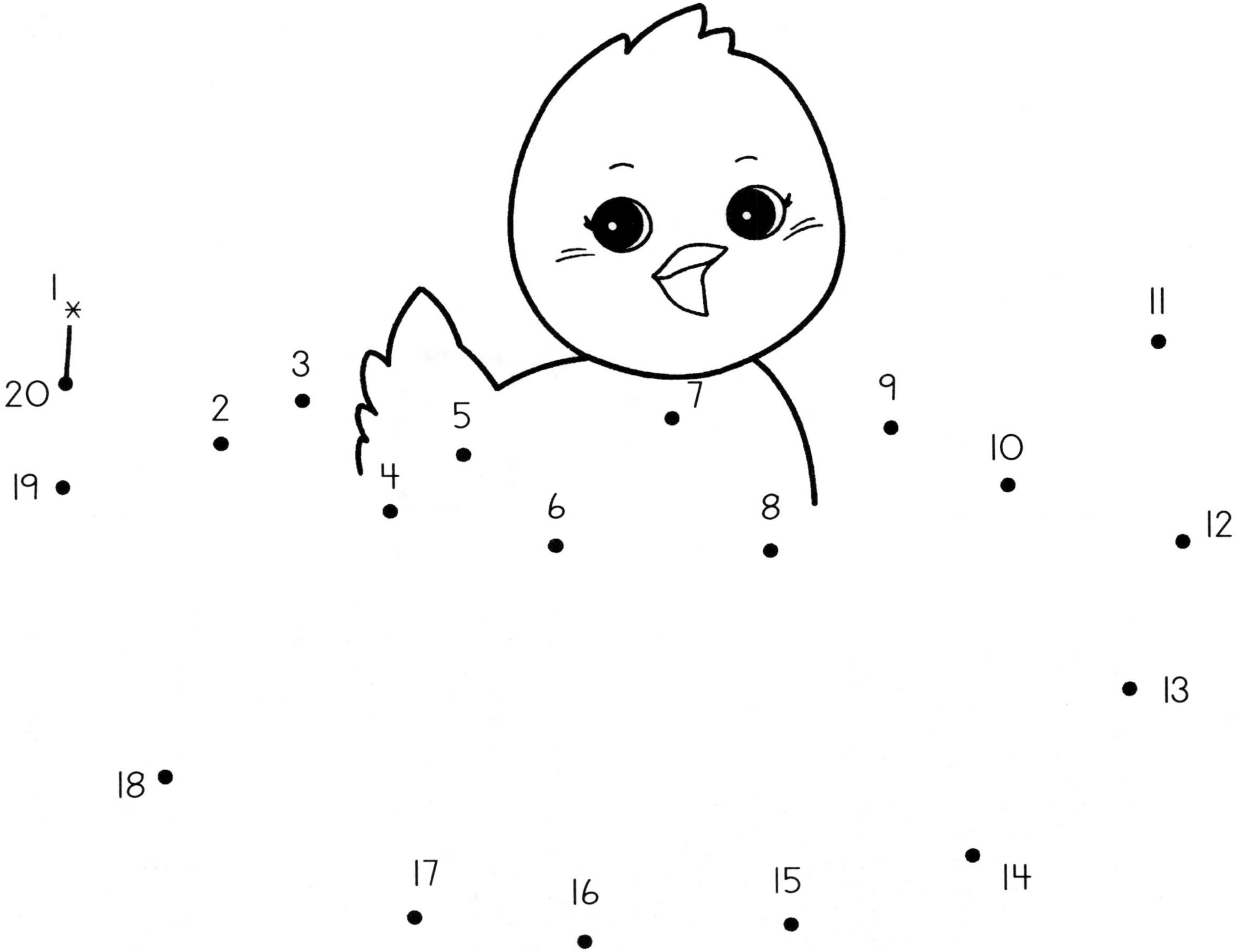

I see a chick.

My Dough Letter Book

By _____

1. Draw your dough letters.

My dough letters looked like this.

1. Write the missing letters.

I can read the letters in my soup.

1. Put the steps in order. Write 1, 2, 3, or 4.

This is how I made my dough letters.

1. Circle the letters that you made.

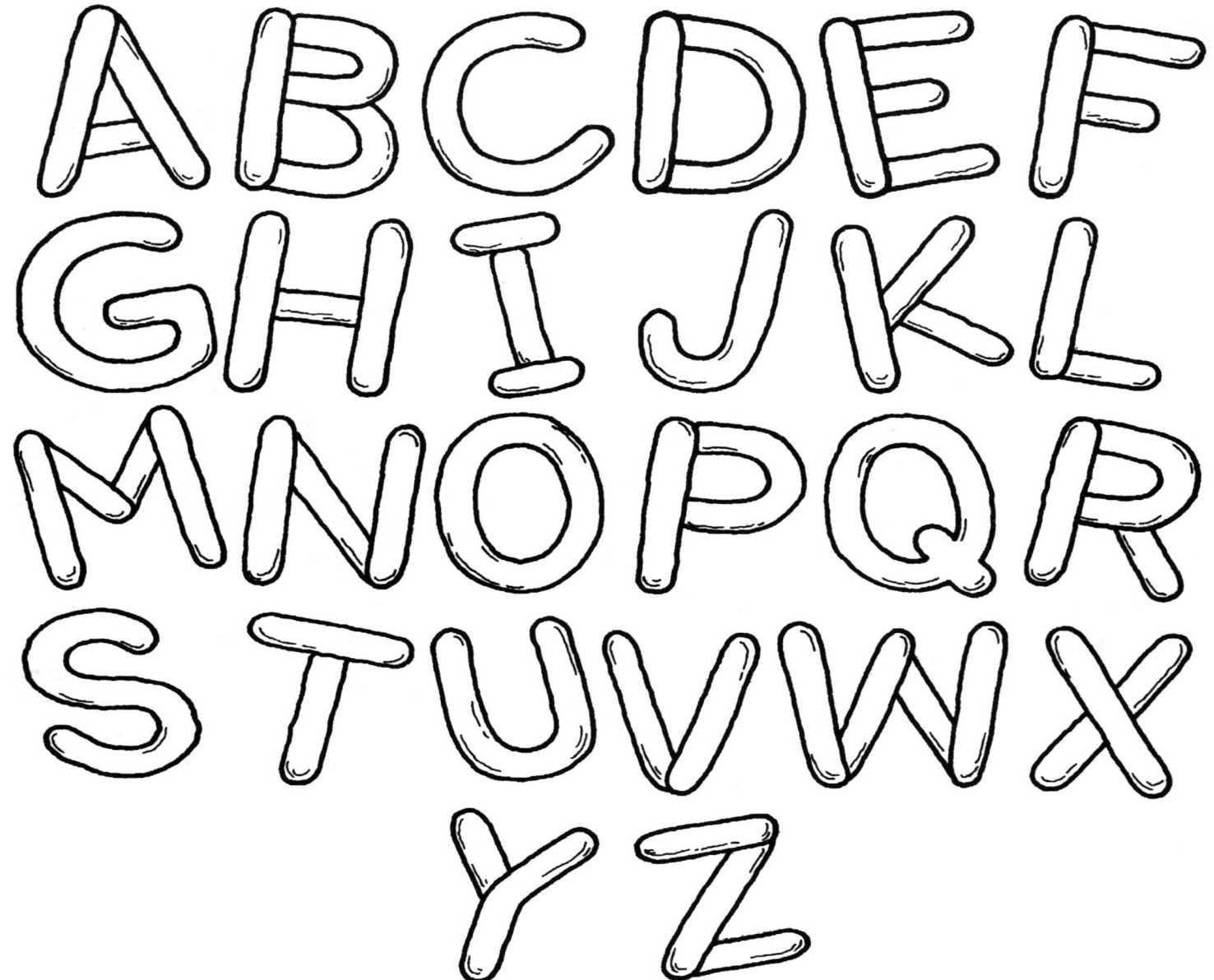

I made these letters with my dough.

1. Read the rhyme.

Sticks, sticks
All in a row.
Sticks, sticks
Made of dough.

First I'll bend them,
Then I'll bake.
Then I'll eat
The letters I make!

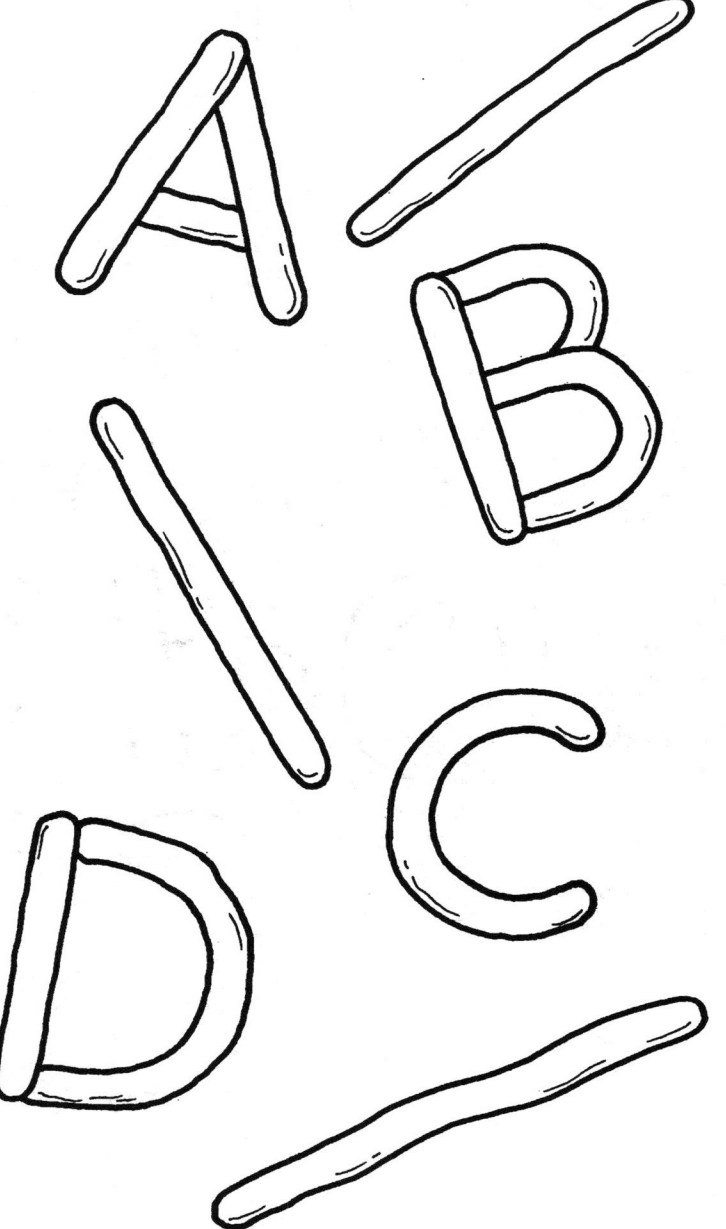

My Rainbow Book

By _____

1. Draw a rainbow.

This is my rainbow.

1. Read.
2. Color the dough.

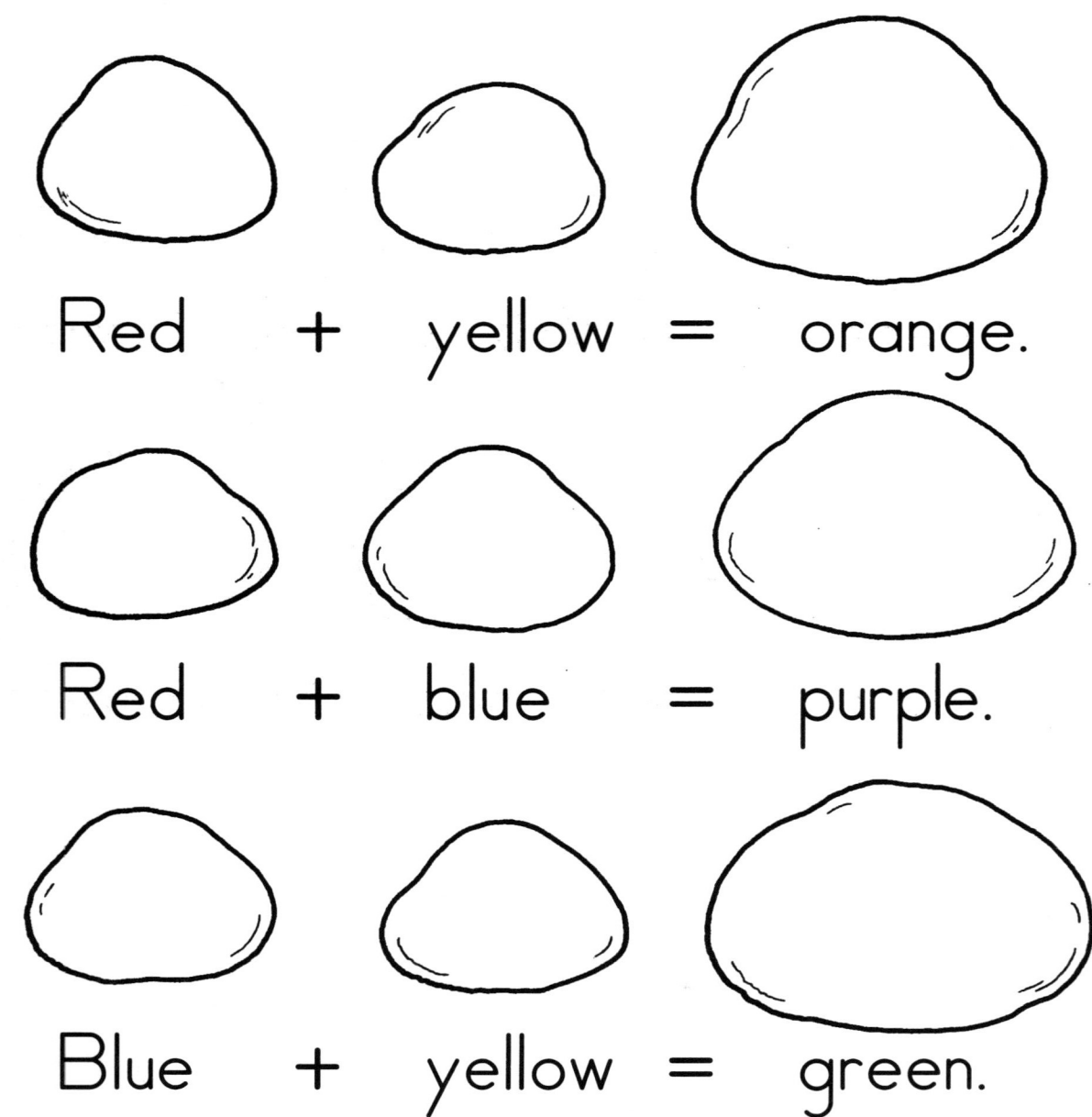

1. Start at the *.
2. Connect the dots.

I see a rainbow.

1. Sing the song.

Color Surprise

Sung to: "Mary Had a Little Lamb"

Red and yellow, mix, mix, mix.
Mix, mix, mix. Mix, mix, mix.
Red and yellow, mix, mix, mix—
What a nice surprise!

Now it's orange, mix, mix, mix.
Mix, mix, mix. Mix, mix, mix.
Now it's orange, mix, mix, mix—
Right before my eyes!

1. Read the rhyme.

I looked in the sky,
And what did I see?
A colorful rainbow
High above me.

My Eggshell Art Book

By _____

1. Read the rhyme.
2. Color the eggs.

We colored eggs red.

We colored eggs blue.

We colored eggs yellow.

We colored green eggs, too!

1. Glue torn paper to make a picture.

I made an eggshell picture.
It looked like this.

2

1. Read the numeral.
2. Draw eggs to match in each basket.

I can count the eggs.

1. Read the poem.
2. Write the rhyming words.

I found an egg
Out in the sun.
How many eggs?
I have _____.

I found one more egg
By my shoe.
How many eggs?
I have _____.

I found one more egg
Under the tree.
How many eggs?
I have _____.

1. Color the last egg to finish the pattern.

I made patterns with eggs!

My Handy Puppet Book

By _____

© 1998 Totline® Publications
(reproducible) p68

1. Trace around your hand.
2. Draw a stick and a face.

© 1998 Totline® Publications
(reproducible) p69

My hand puppet looked like this.

1

1. Trace your hand.
2. Make a picture.
3. Write about it.

I made my hand into a _____.

© 1998 Totline® Publications
(reproducible) p70

1. Put the steps in order. Write 1, 2, 3, or 4.

This is how I made my puppet.

1. Read the rhyme.
2. Cross out one puppet.
3. How many puppets are left? Circle the number.

Four little puppets
Happy as can be.
One went home,
Then there were   5   3   2   1.

1. Read the rhyme.
2. Draw a picture to show what your puppet can do.

My puppet can dance.
My puppet can sing.
My puppet can do
Most anything!

My Lei Book

By _____

© 1998 Totline® Publications
My Lei Book
(reproducible) p74

1. What colors are in your lei?

Use those colors to color the picture.

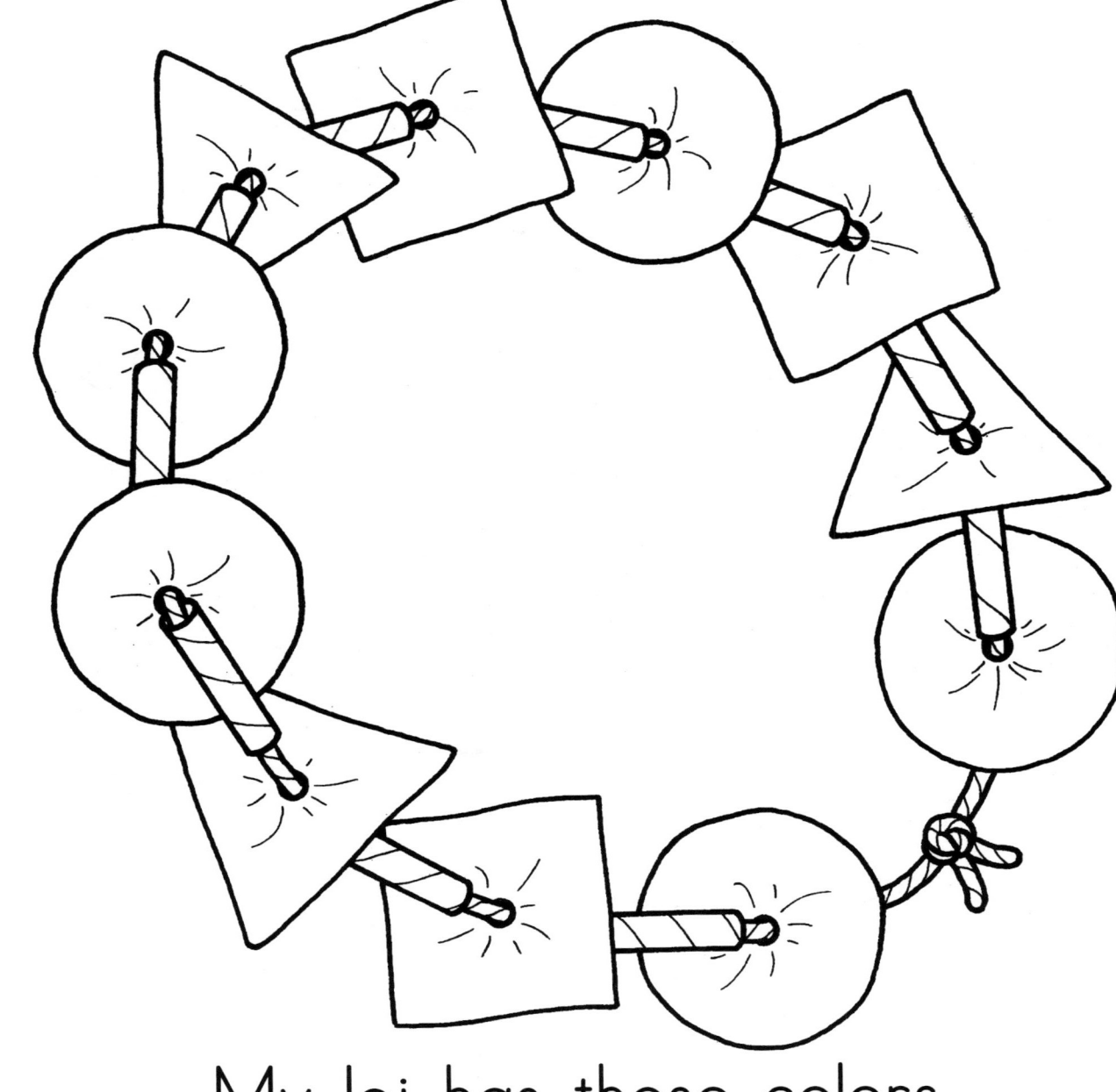

My lei has these colors.

1. Put the steps in order. Write 1, 2, 3, or 4.

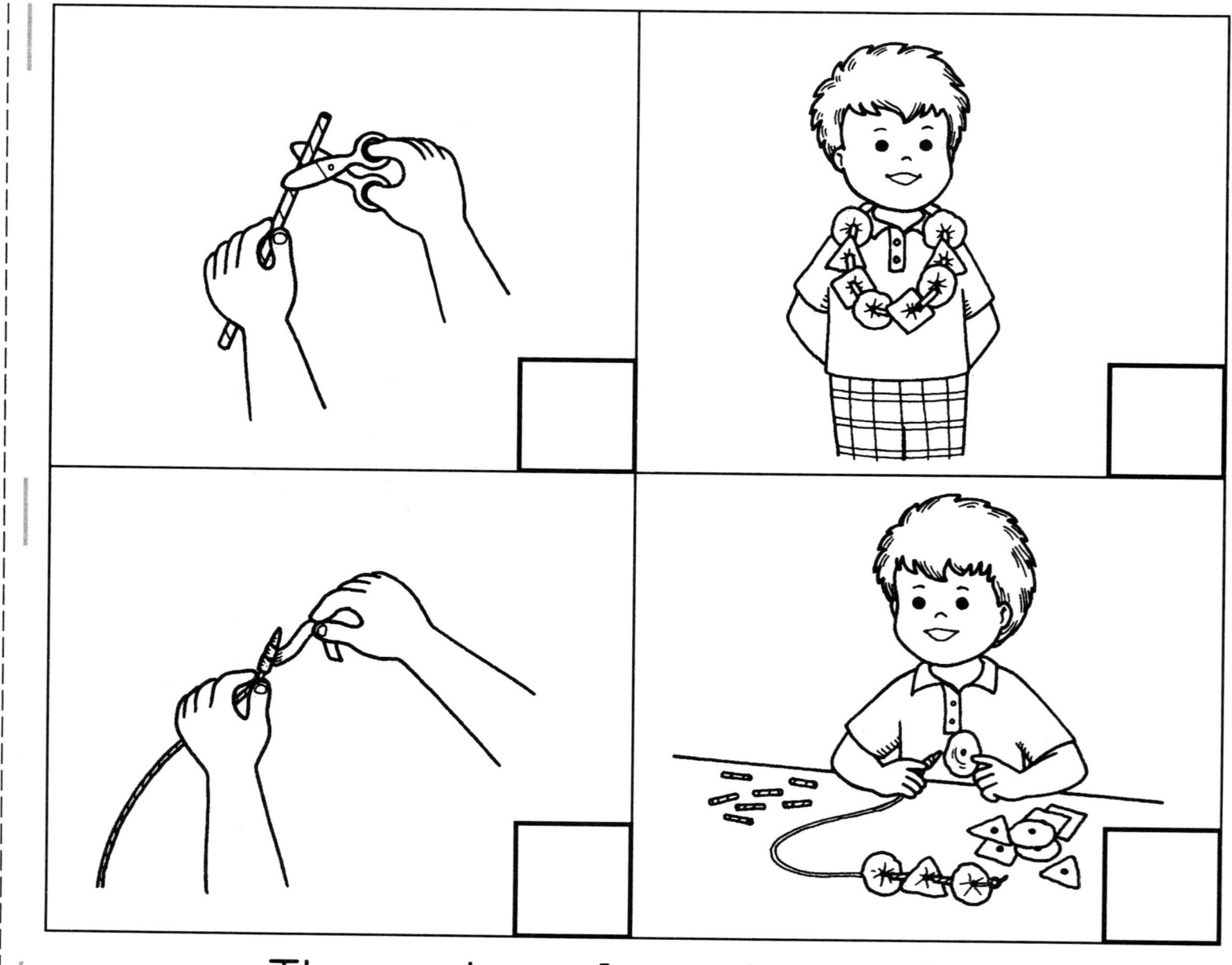

This is how I made my lei.

1. Count the flowers in your lei. Write the number.

2. Count the straws in your lei. Write the number.

My lei has ___ flowers.

My lei has ___ straws.

1. Color the pictures to make a pattern.

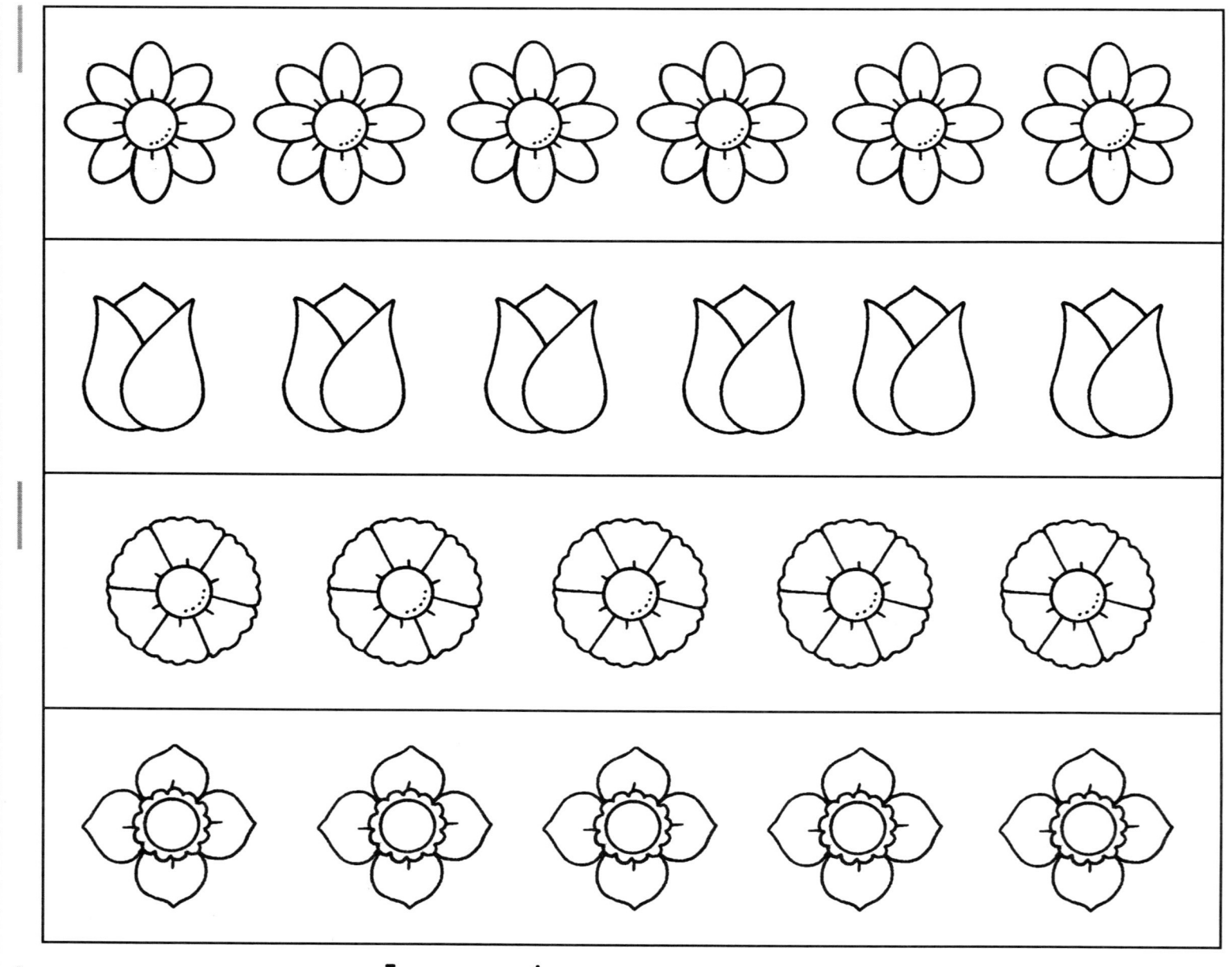

I made a pattern.

1. Read the rhyme.

I have a flower necklace.
My necklace is a lei.
When I wear my necklace,
I have a happy day!

My Paint Mixing Book

By _____

© 1998 Totline® Publications
(reproducible) p80

1. What colors did you use?
2. Color the paint.

I painted with these colors.

1. What's your favorite color of paint? Write the color word.
2. Color the picture.

My favorite paint color is _____.

1. How many pictures did you paint today? Circle the number.
2. Write the number.

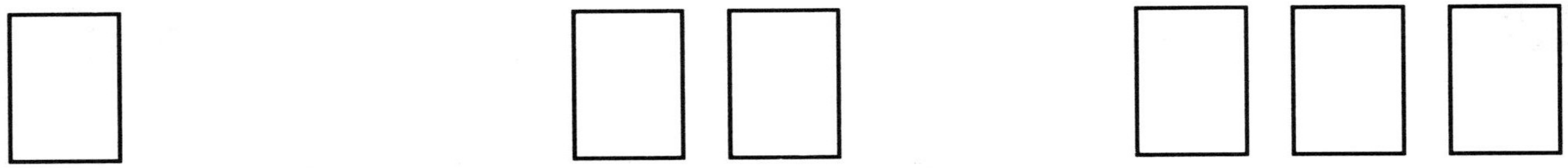

1   2   3

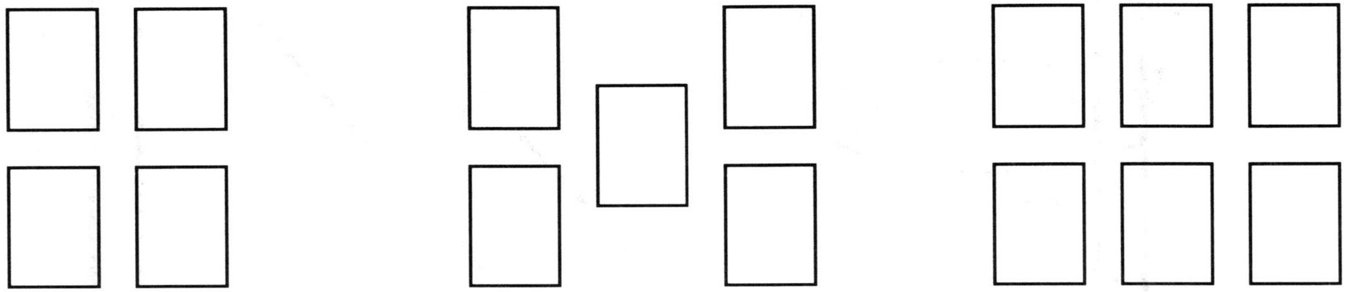

4   5   6

I painted _____ pictures today.

1. Draw a purple picture.

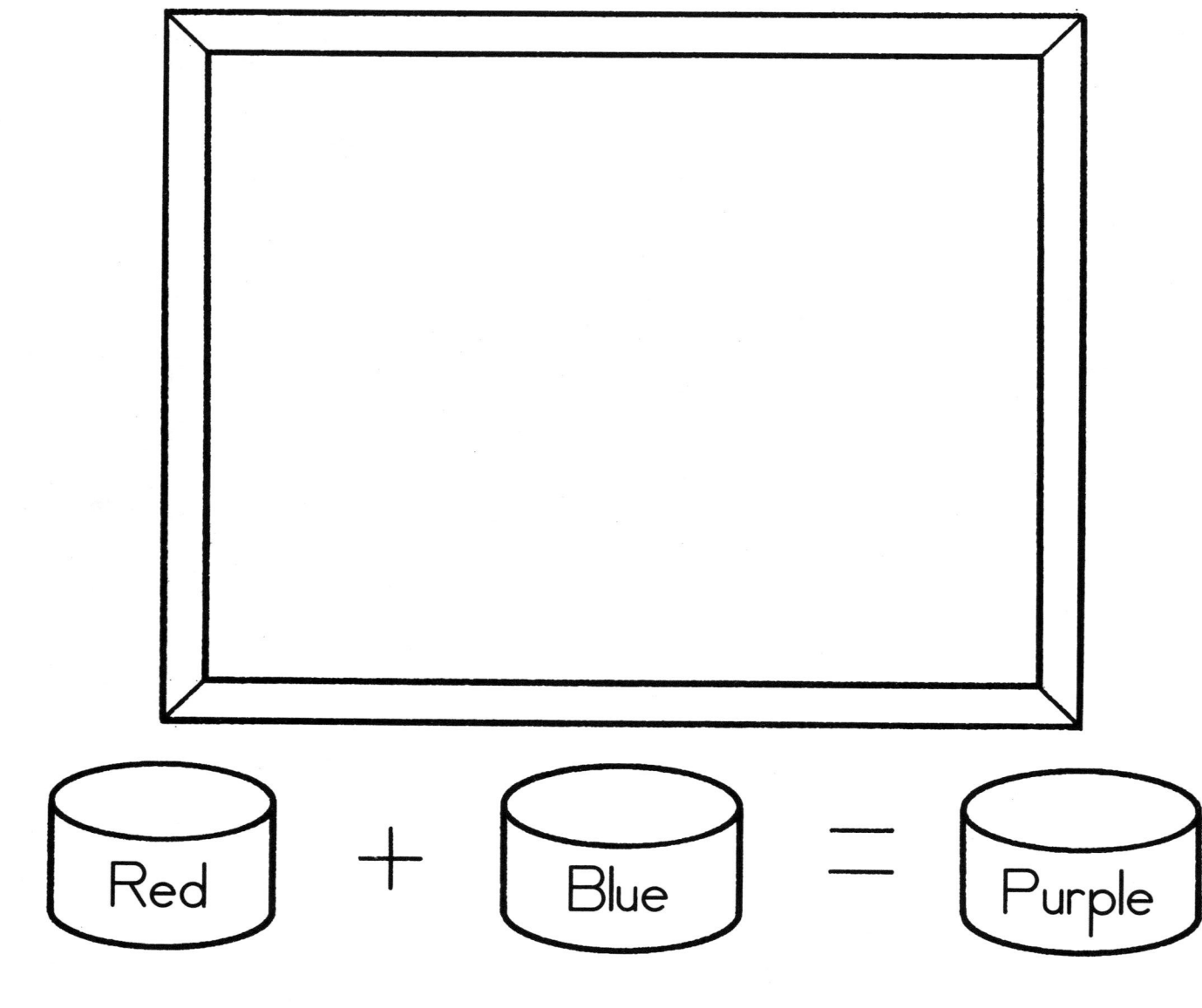

I know how to make purple.

1. Sing the song.

Painting Is Fun

Sung to: "The Farmer in the Dell"

I painted pictures today.
I painted pictures today.
Painting is fun, hooray, hooray!
I painted pictures today.

I made lots of colors today.
I made lots of colors today.
Purple and green, hooray, hooray!
I painted pictures today.

My Painted Paper Egg Book

By _____

© 1998 Totline® Publications
(reproducible) p86

1. Draw a picture of your eggs.
2. How many did you make? Write the number.

I made _____ paper eggs.

1. Circle the matching eggs.
2. Color the picture.

These eggs match.

1. Start at the *.
2. Connect the dots.
3. Color the picture.

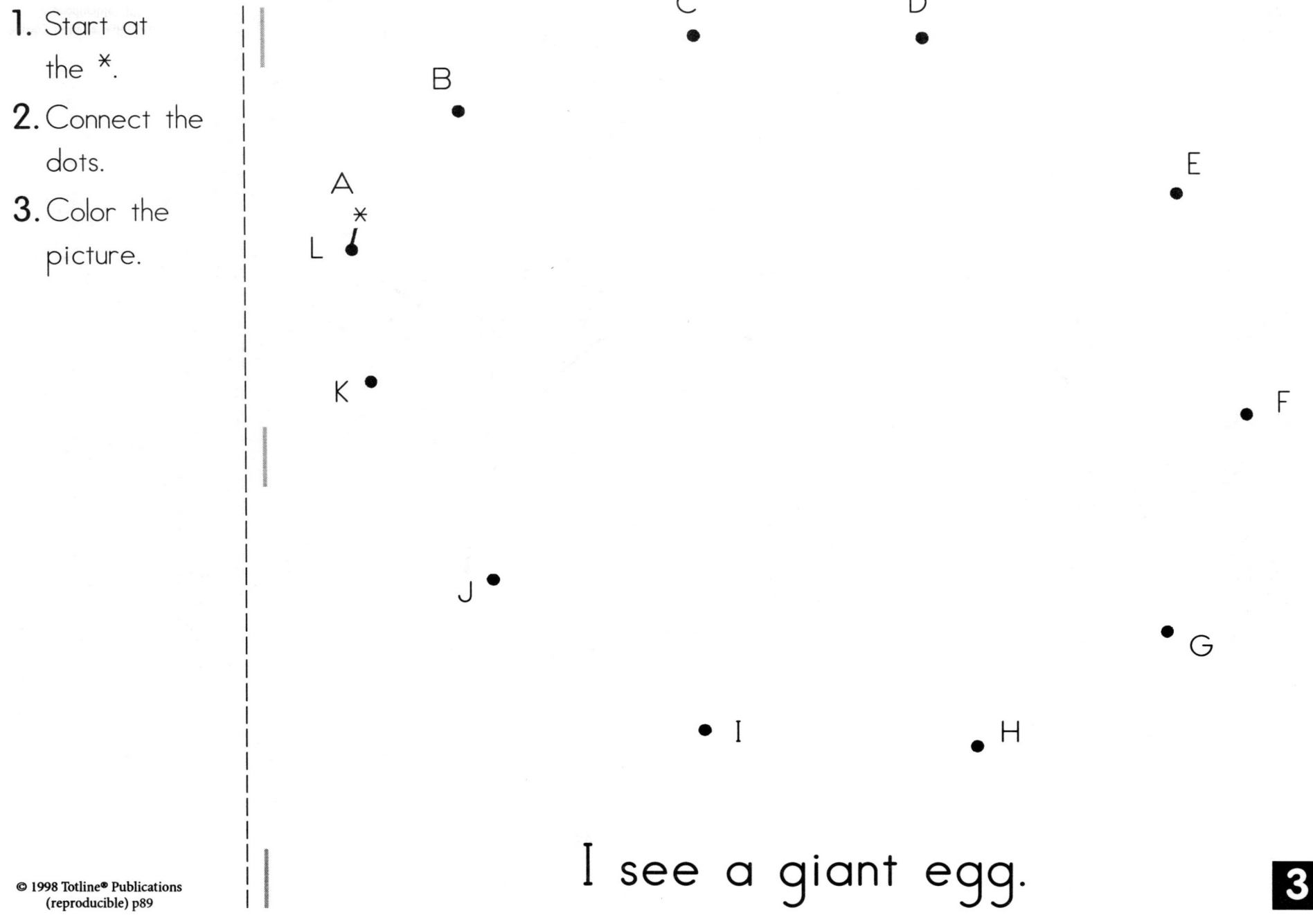

I see a giant egg.

1. Draw a baby animal in the egg.
2. Fill in the blank.

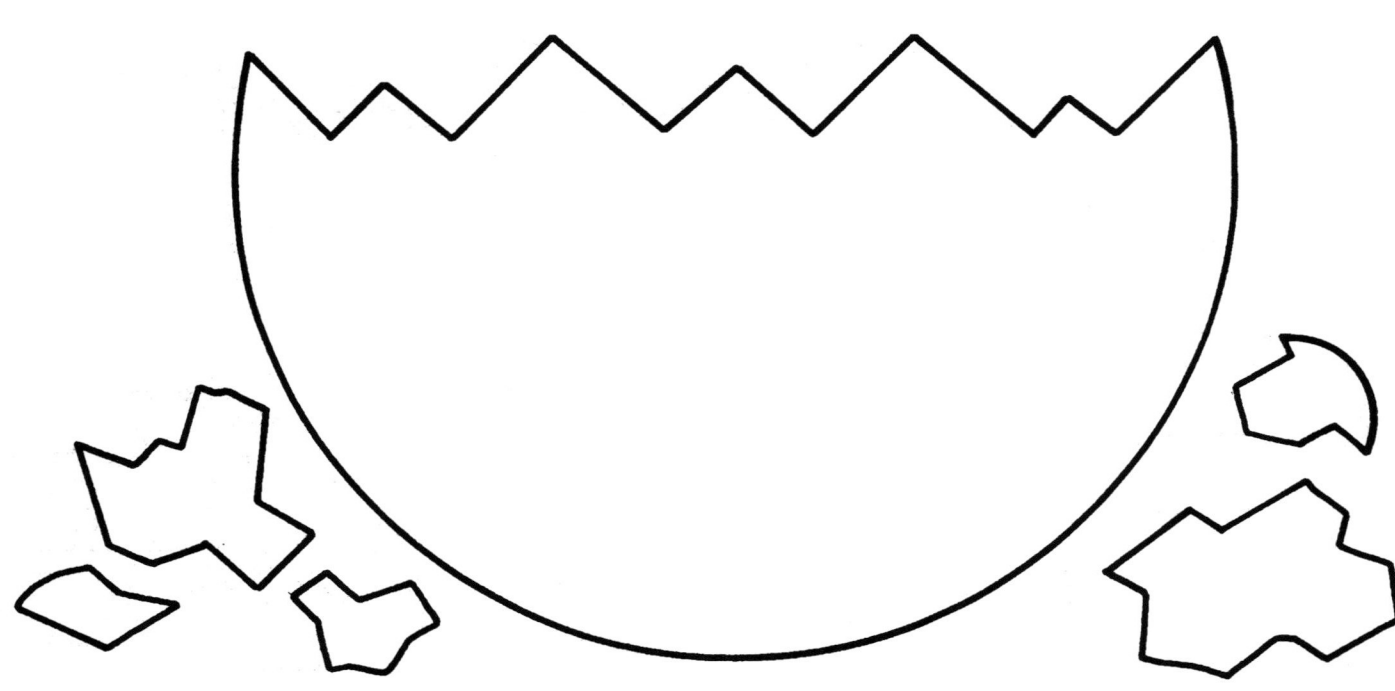

Inside is a _____.

1. Read the rhyme.
2. Color one egg red, one blue, and the other the color of your choice.

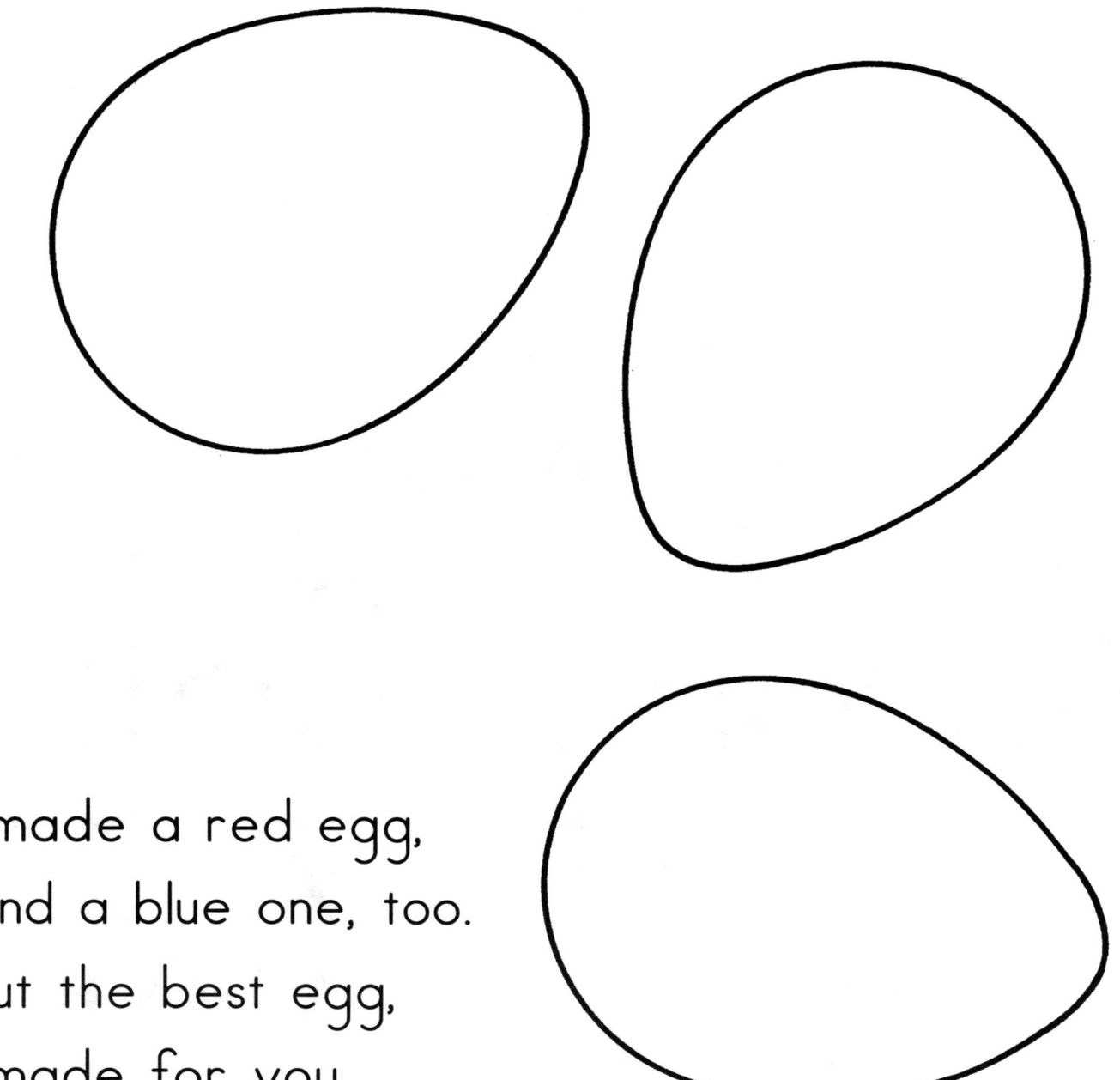

I made a red egg,
And a blue one, too.
But the best egg,
I made for you.

My Paper Bag Puppet Book

By _____

© 1998 Totline® Publications
(reproducible) p92

1. Draw your puppet.

My puppet looked like this.

1. Count the puppets.
2. Write the number.
3. Color the puppets.

My puppet has _____ friends.

1. Read the rhyme.
2. Count the puppets.
3. Write the number.

Four little puppets
Sitting in a tree.

One went home,
That left _____.

1. What colors did you use for your puppet? Use those colors to color the crayons.
2. Count the colors.
3. Write the number.

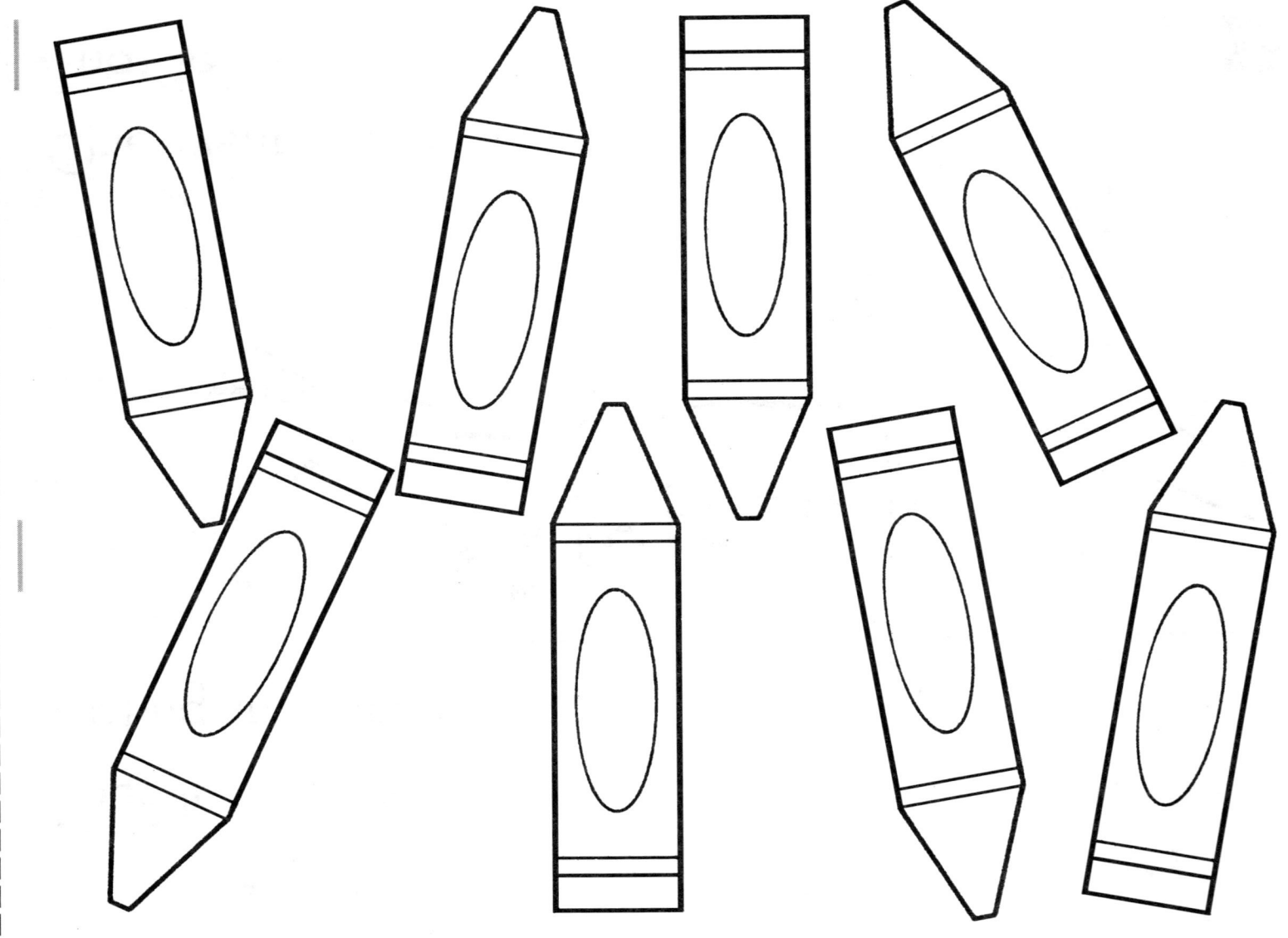

These are the colors of my puppet.
I used _____ colors.

1. Sing the song.
2. Draw a picture of your puppet.

I Have a Little Puppet

Sung to: "The Farmer in the Dell"

I have a little puppet,
It is my friend.
I can make it dance and jump,
And bow with a bend.

I can sing this song.

© 1998 Totline® Publications
(reproducible) p97

My Paper Cup Flower Book

By _____

1. Color the flower.

My flower looks like this.

1. How many petals does each flower have? Write the number.
2. Color the flowers.

Flowers have petals.

1. Read the number on each vase. Draw that many flowers.

I put flowers in the vase.

1. Read the words.
2. Color the cups.

Some cups are red.
Some cups are blue.

1. Draw a picture of flowers.

I made these flowers
Just for you!

My Paper Plate Hat Book

By _____

1. Draw yourself wearing your hat.

I made a hat from a paper plate.

© 1998 Totline® Publications
(reproducible) p105

1. Count the hats.
2. Write the number.
3. Color the hats.

I see ____ hats.

1. Draw a line to connect the matching hats.

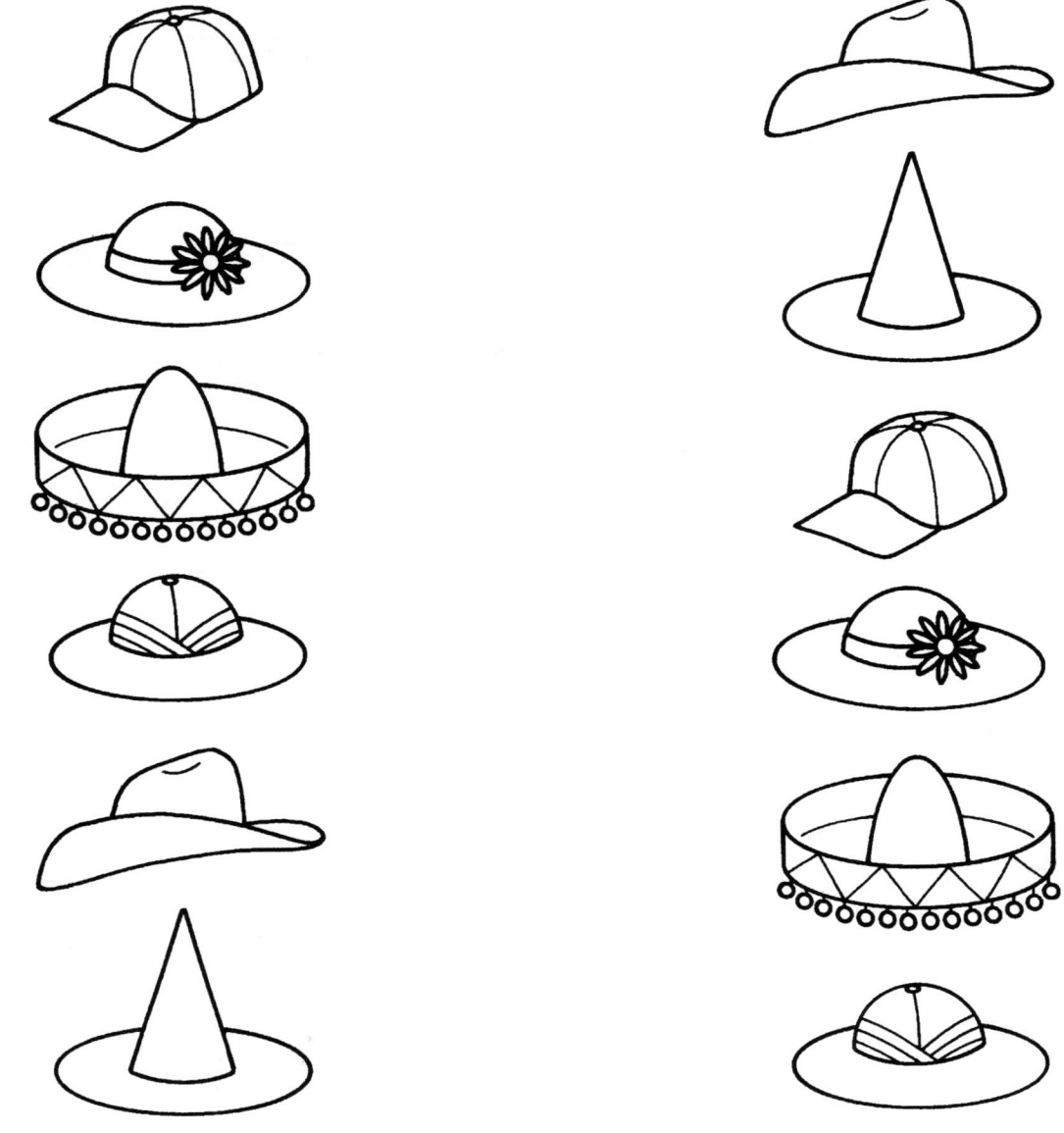

These hats match.

1. Draw hats on the kids.

These kids have hats.

1. Read the rhyme.
2. Write the color words.
3. Color the hat.

I love hats.
Yes, I do.
I love hats
Colored blue.

I love hats.
That's what I said.
I love hats
Colored red.

I love hats!

My Paper Weaving Book

By _____

© 1998 Totline® Publications
(reproducible) p110

1. Put the steps in order. Write 1, 2, 3, or 4.

This is how I made my mat.

1. How many paper strips did you use? Write the number.
2. Color the strips.

I used _____ paper strips.
They are these colors.

1. Color the picture. Make it look like your mat.

My mat looked like this.

1. How will you use your mat? Draw a picture.

I like to use my mat.

1. Sing the song.

I Am Weaving

Sung to: "Frère Jacques"

I am weaving.
I am weaving.
Watch me go.
Watch me go.
Over and under.
Over and under.
Fast and slow.
Fast and slow.

My Rainy Day Book

By _____

© 1998 Totline® Publications
(reproducible) p116

1. Put the steps in order. Write 1, 2, 3, or 4.

This is how I made my rainy day picture.

1. Draw flowers on the stems.

Rain helps flowers grow.

2

© 1998 Totline® Publications
(reproducible) p118

1. Draw a rain picture.
2. Where is the rain falling? Finish the sentence.

It is raining on the _____.

1. Count the raindrops in each window.
2. Circle the correct number.

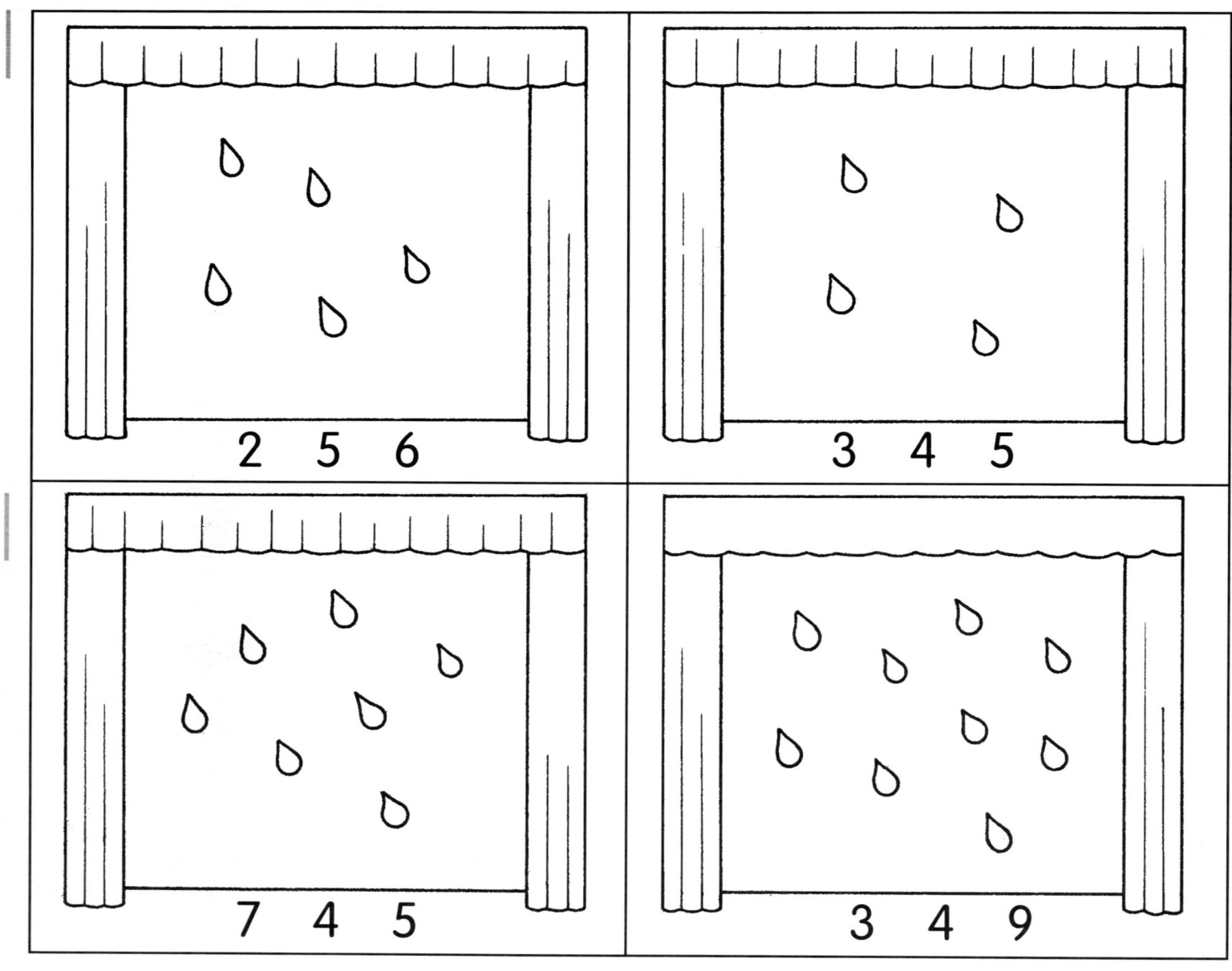

I can count raindrops.

1. Color the pictures that begin with the R sound.

These are "R" words.

My Salt Picture Book

By _____

1. Put the steps in order. Write 1, 2, 3, or 4.

This is how I made my salt picture.

1. Draw a winter picture.
2. Color the picture.
3. Glue on some salt.

Salt looks like snow.

1. Count the salt shakers.
2. Circle the correct number.

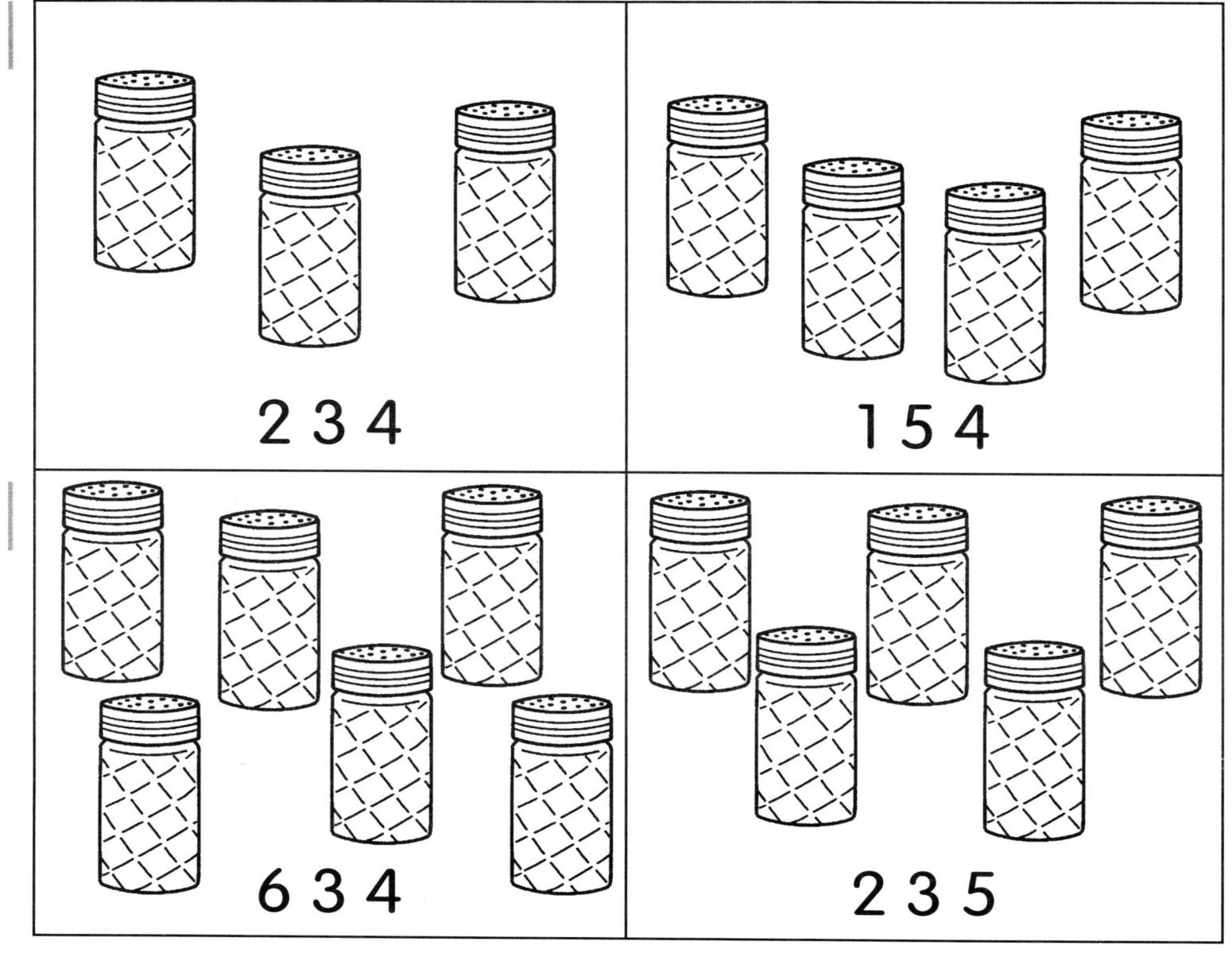

I can count the salt shakers.

1. Read the rhyme.
2. Color the pictures.

Rainbow Foods

If I had some colored salt,
This is what I'd do.
I'd sprinkle salt upon my eggs,
And turn my breakfast blue.

My popcorn would be purple,
My sandwich I'd turn red,
And when I was all full of food,
I'd hop into my bed.

1. Sing the song.
2. Color the picture.

Winter Pictures

Sung to: "Sing a Song of Sixpence"

Sing a song of salt,
Sprinkle it here and there.
Making winter pictures,
Cold frost everywhere.

When my pictures's done,
I hang it up to dry.
My picture looks just like
A frosty winter sky!

My Shape Lacing Book

By _____

1. Draw your shape.
2. Color the picture.

My shape looked like this.

© 1998 Totline® Publications
(reproducible) p129

1. Circle the shortest shoestring.

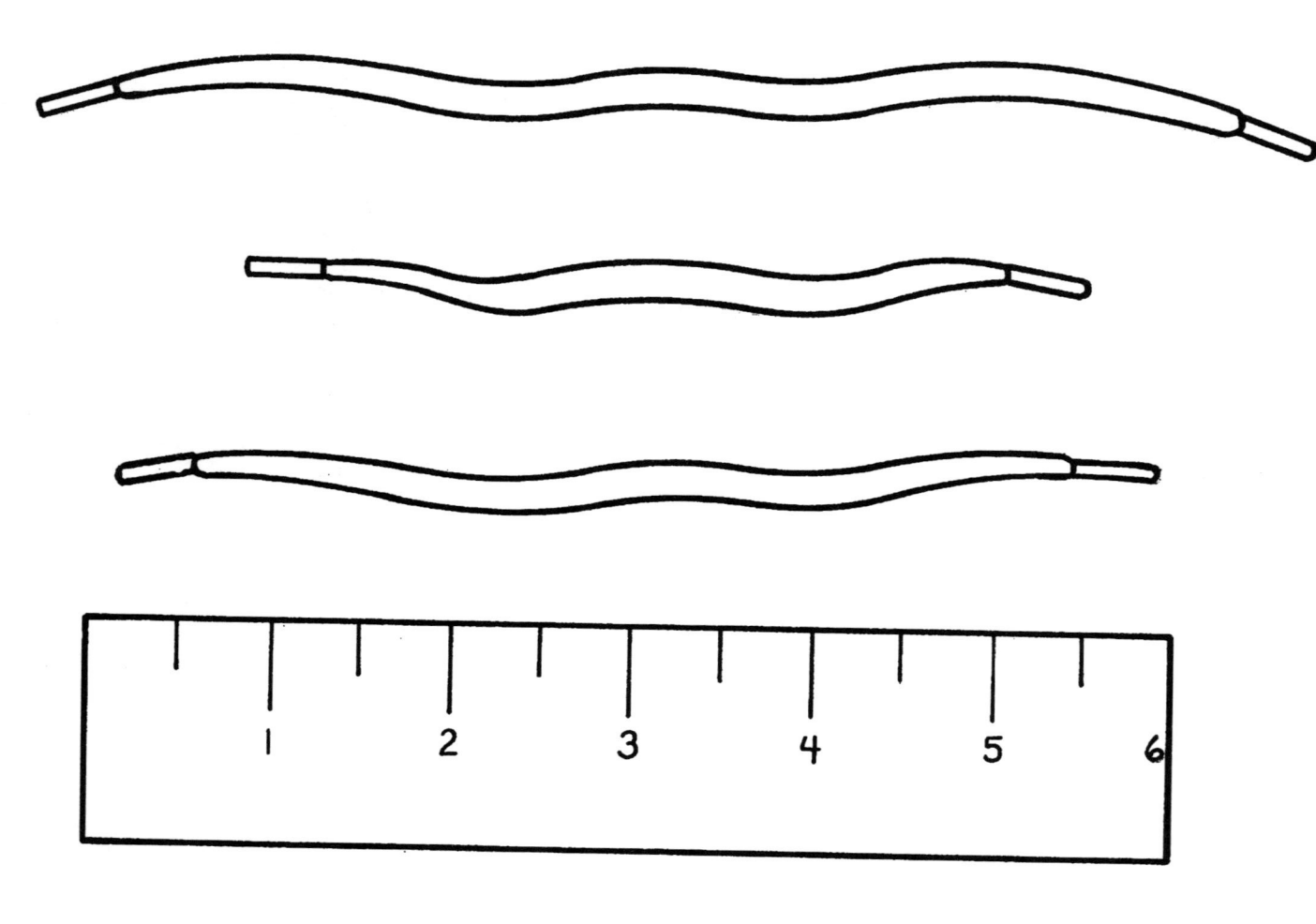

I can measure.

1. Start at the *.
2. Connect the dots.

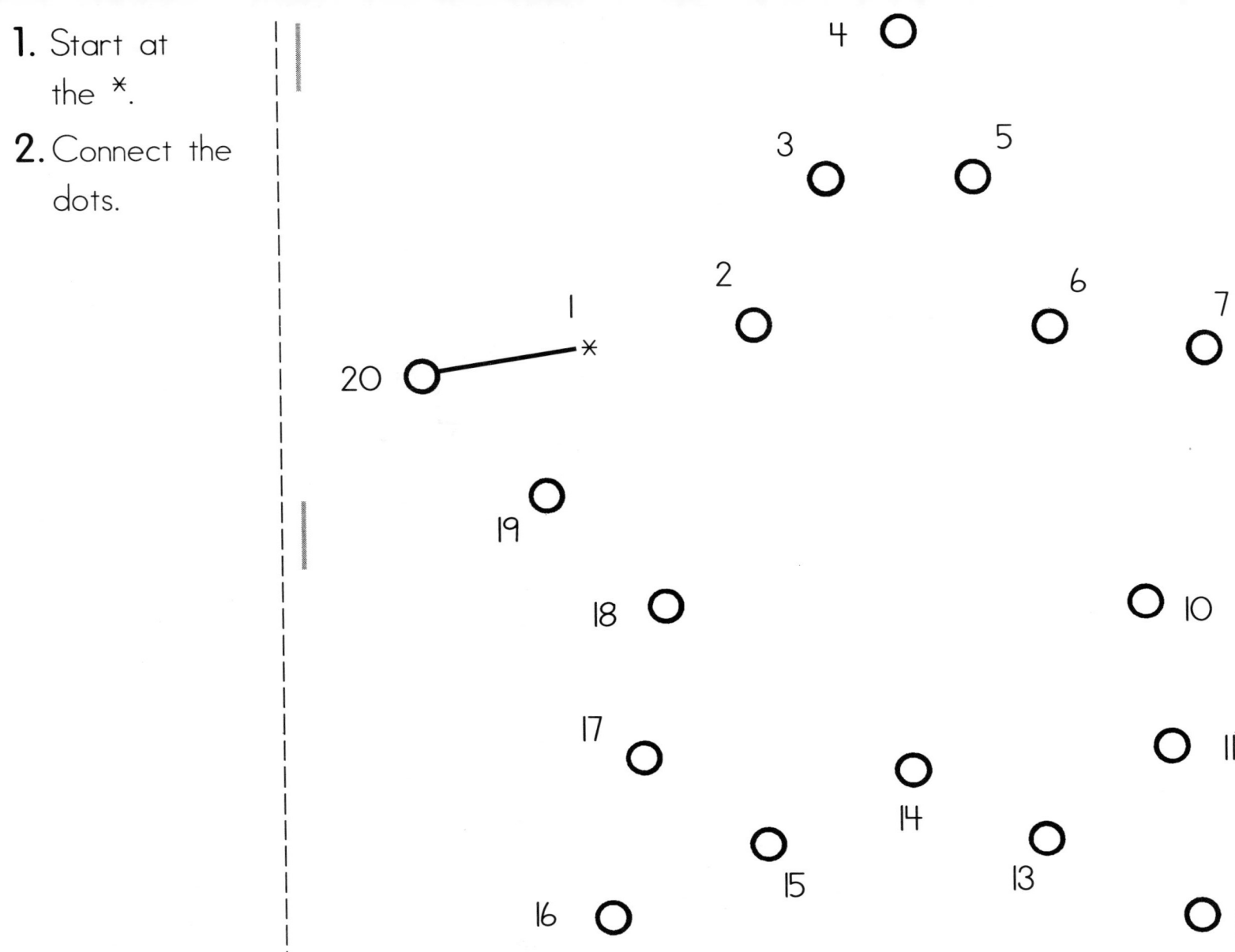

I see a star.

1. Count the laced shapes.
2. Circle the correct number.

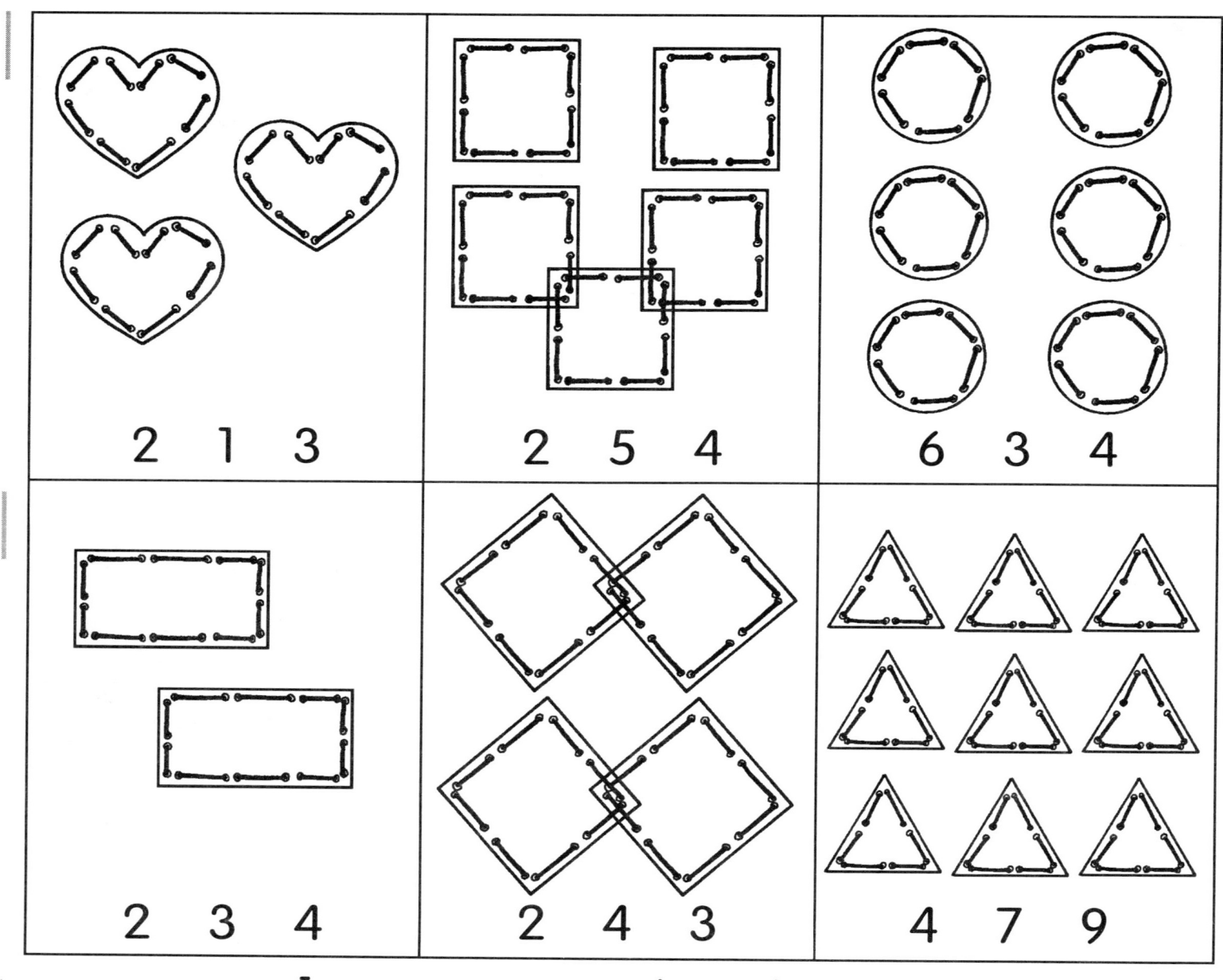

I can count the shapes.

1. Count the shapes.
2. Write the number.

I see _____ ●.   I see _____ ▲.

I see _____ ■.   I see _____ ▬.

My Heart Picture Book

By _____

1. Draw your heart picture.
2. How many hearts are in your picture?
3. Write the number.

My heart picture looked like this.
I have _____ hearts in my picture.

1. Draw a heart animal.
2. What kind of animal did you draw? Finish the sentence.

My heart animal is a _____.

1. How many hearts are in each picture? Write the number.

I see _____ hearts.

I see _____ hearts.

1. Read the numeral.
2. Draw that many hearts in each box.

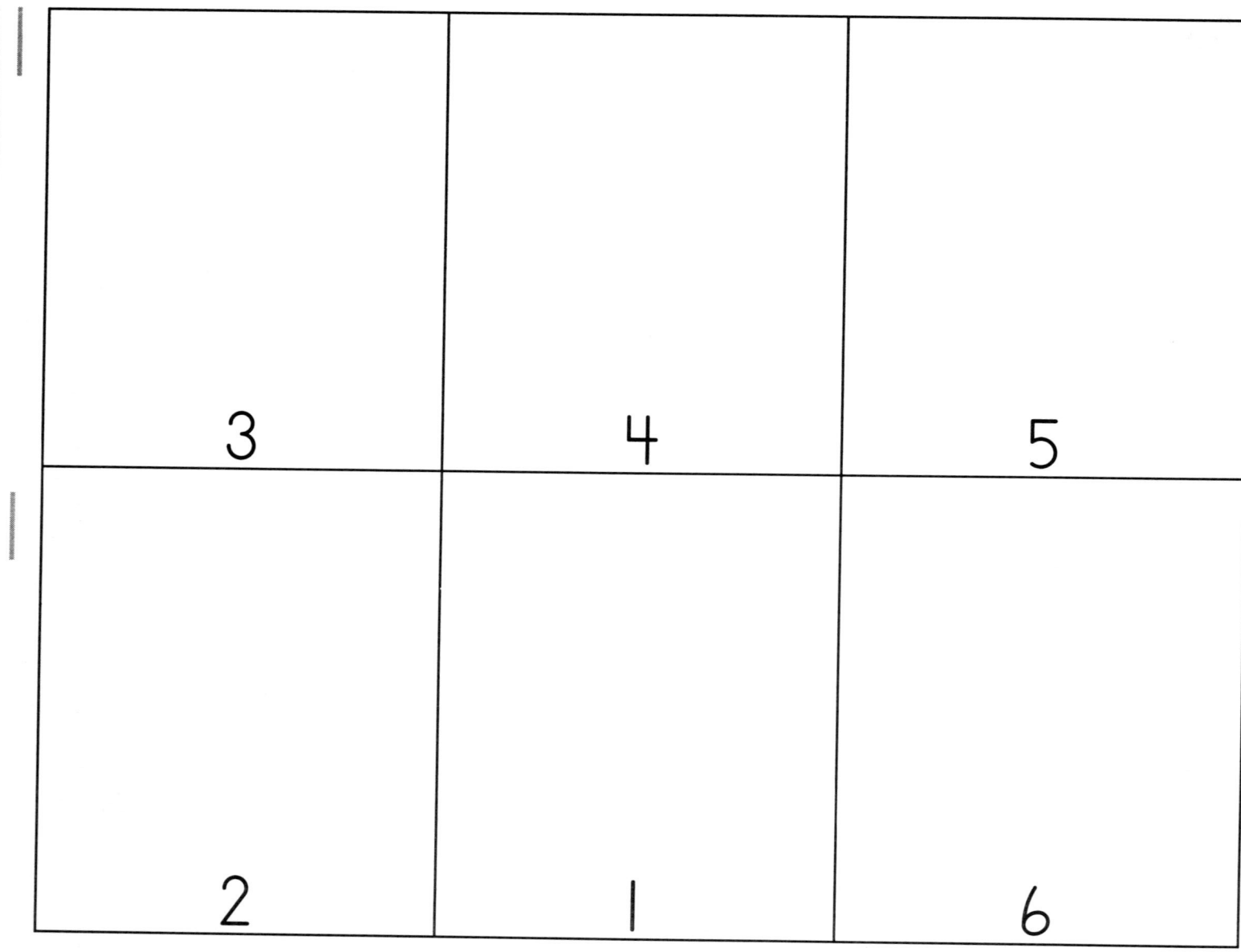

I can draw and count hearts.

1. Write the numbers in order from 1 to 10.

I can write numbers.

My Tissue Paper Painting Book

By _____

1. What colors did you use? Color the papers to match.

I used these colors.

© 1998 Totline® Publications
(reproducible) p141

1

1. Put the steps in order. Write 1, 2, 3, or 4.

This is how I made my picture.

1. Read each number.
2. Glue that many tissue paper squares in the box.

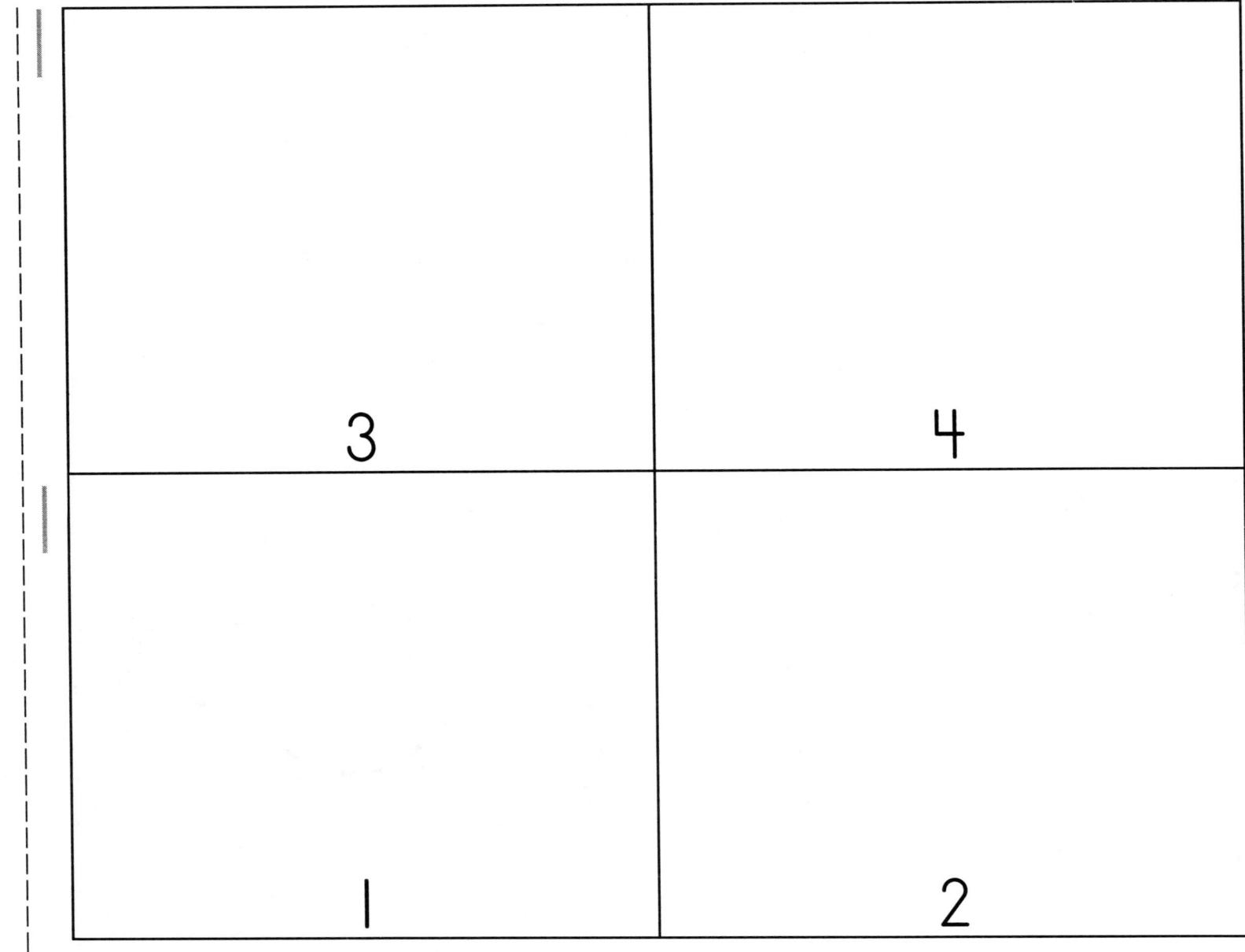

I can count the tissue paper squares.

1. Paint the picture with tissue paper paint. Match the colors.

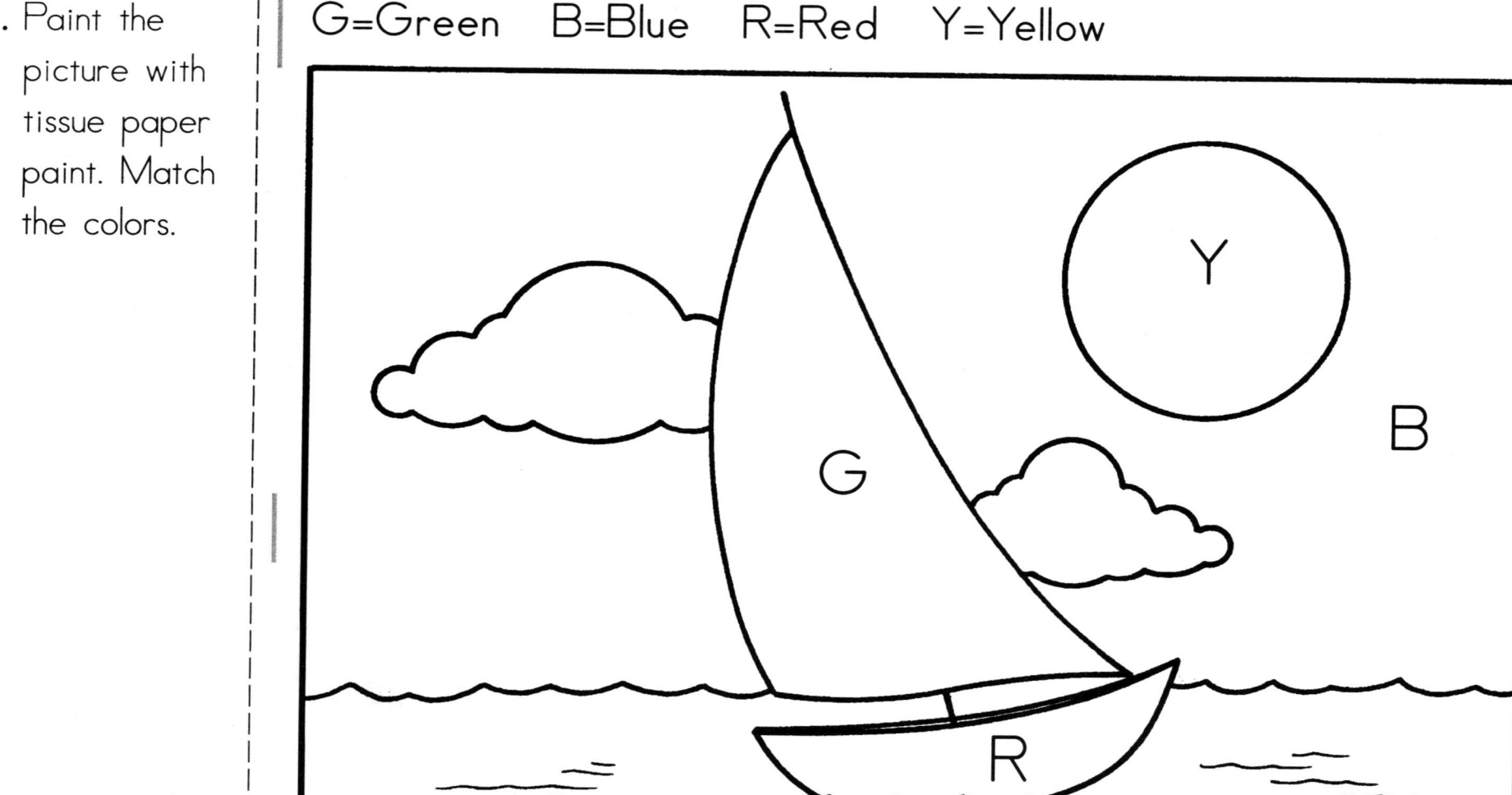

G=Green   B=Blue   R=Red   Y=Yellow

I painted with tissue paper.

4

1. Read the rhyme.
2. Write the number words.
3. Color the picture.

Paper, paper,
So much fun.
Tissue paper pictures,
I made _____.

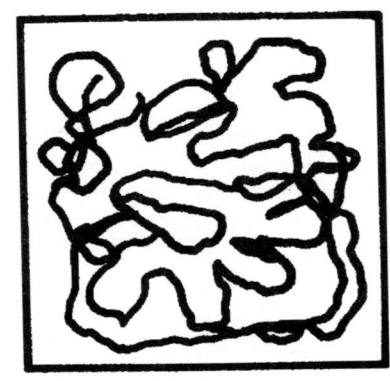

Making pictures
Is fun to do.
Tissue paper pictures,
I made _____.

My Torn Paper Book

By _____

1. What colors of paper did you use?
2. Use those colors to color the paper pieces.

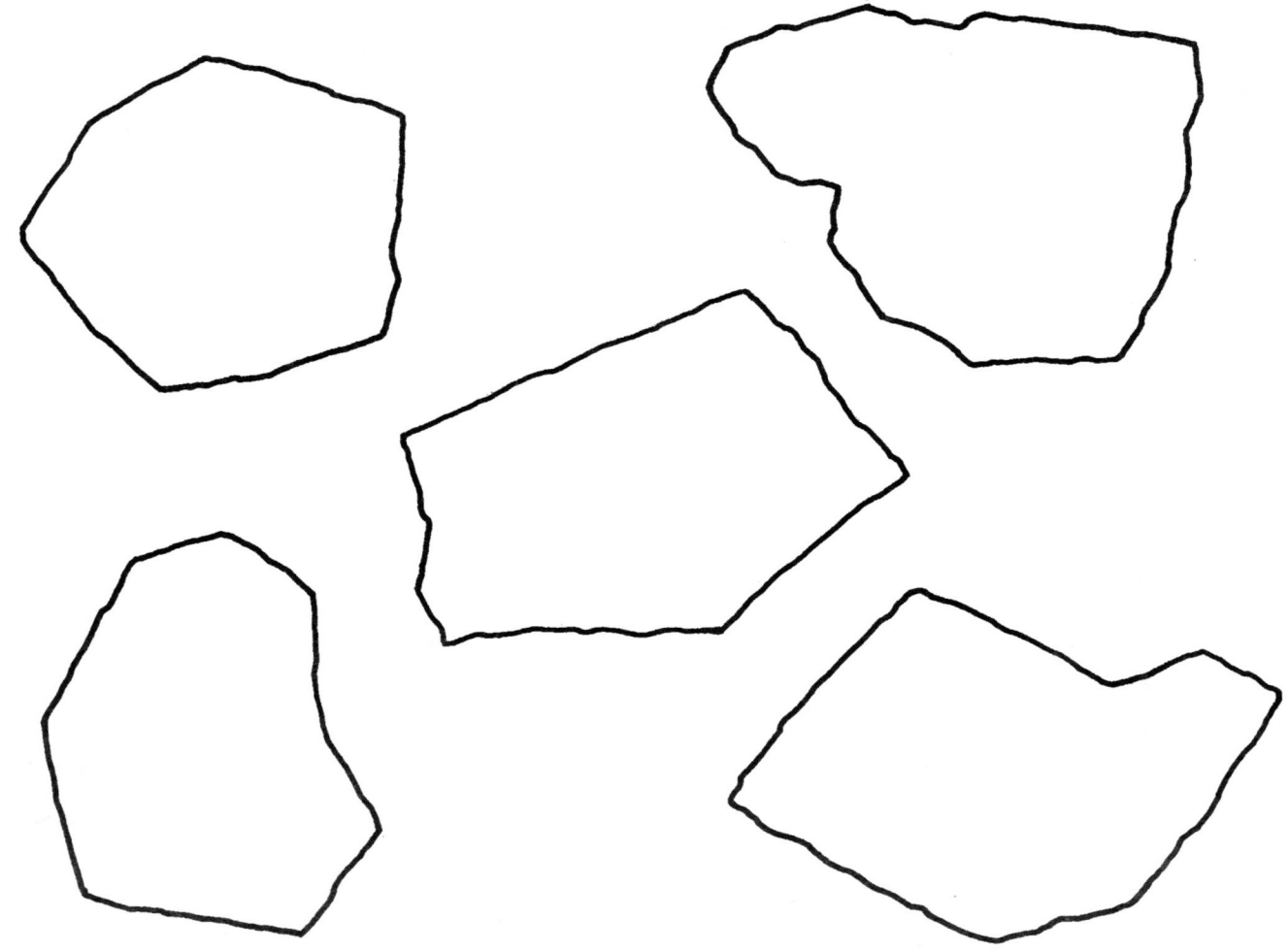

I tore paper.
These are the colors I used.

1. Count the paper pieces in each box.
2. Circle the number.

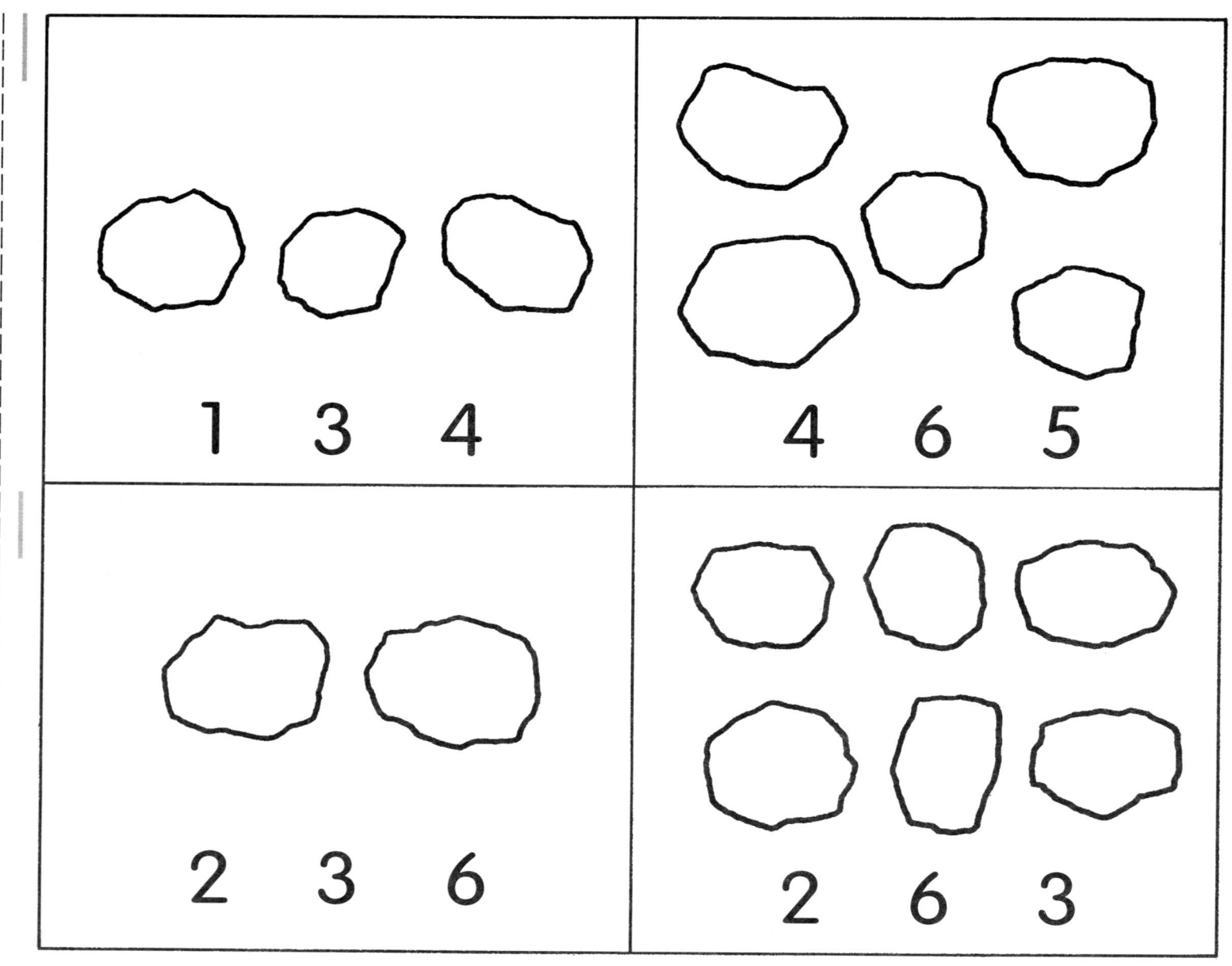

I can count the paper pieces.

1. Circle the paper piece that matches the first one in each row.

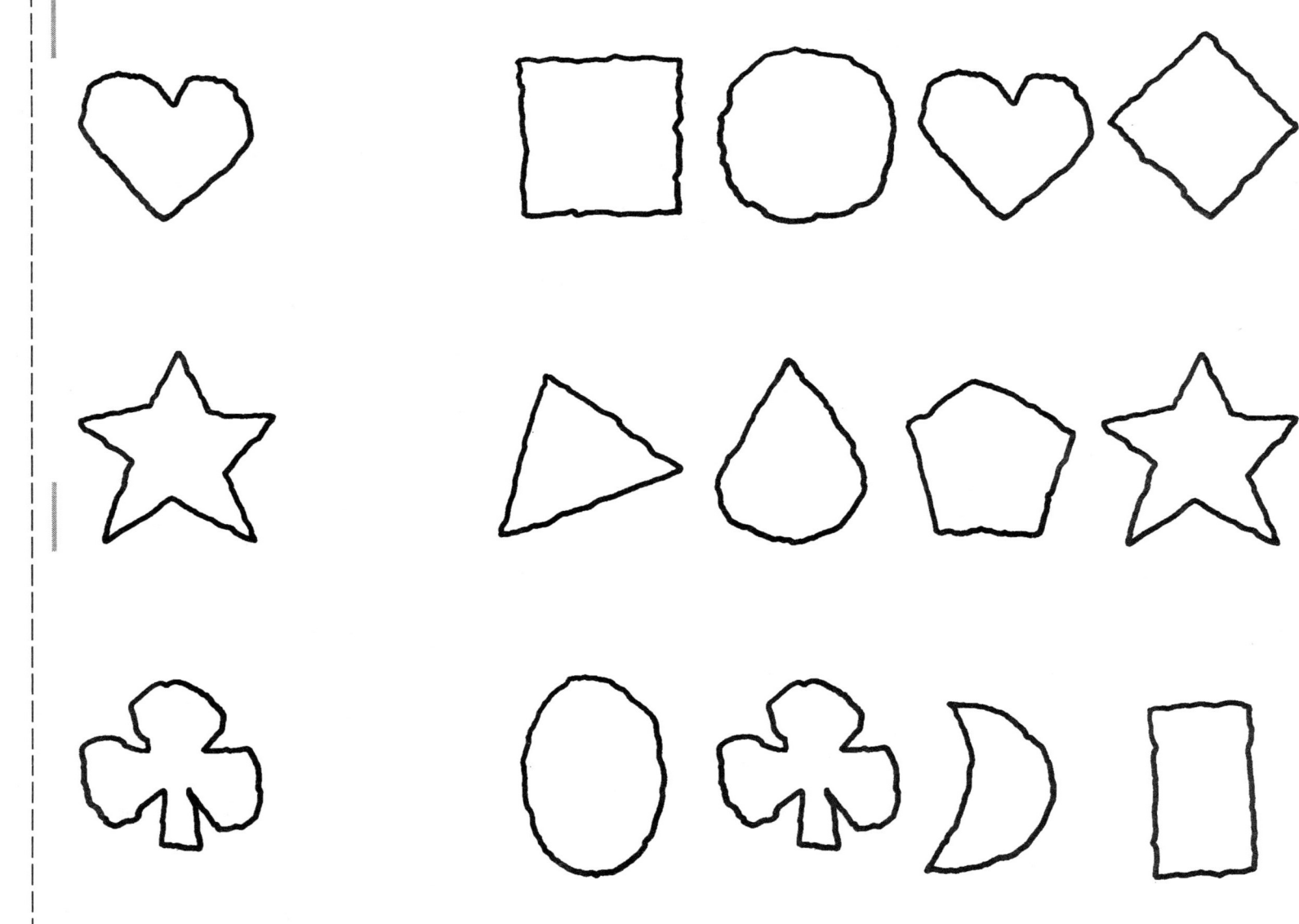

These pieces match the first one.

1. Copy the letters.

I can write letters.

1. Read the rhyme.
2. Color the picture.

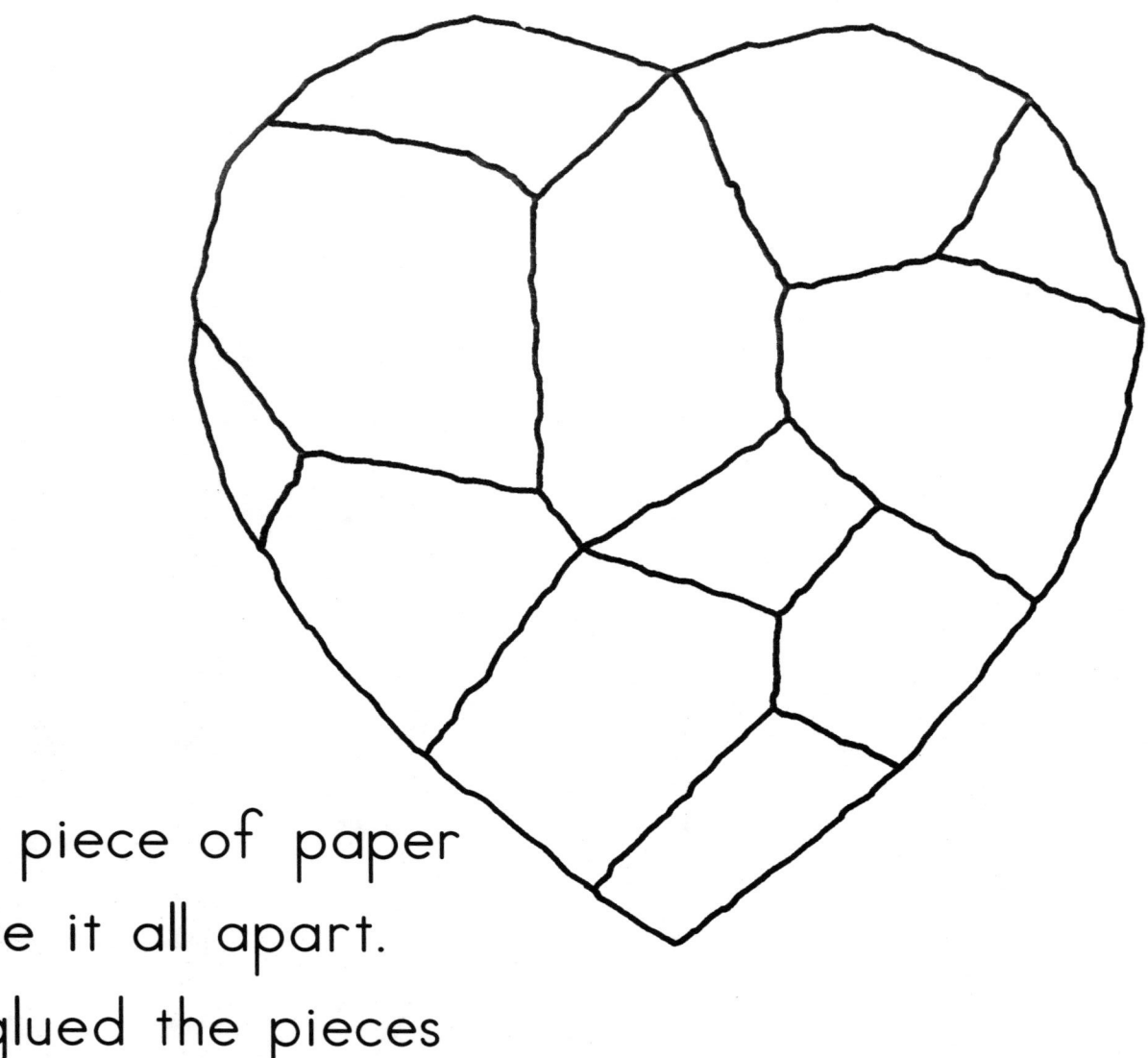

I took a piece of paper
And tore it all apart.
Then I glued the pieces
Into a paper heart.

My Wire Sculpture Book

By _____

1. Draw a picture of your sculpture.

My sculpture looked like this.

1. Draw a line to connect the matching shapes.

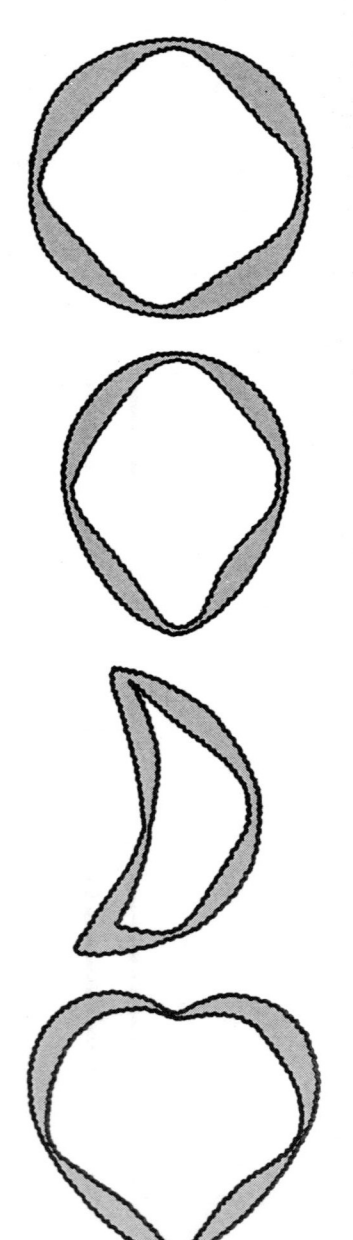
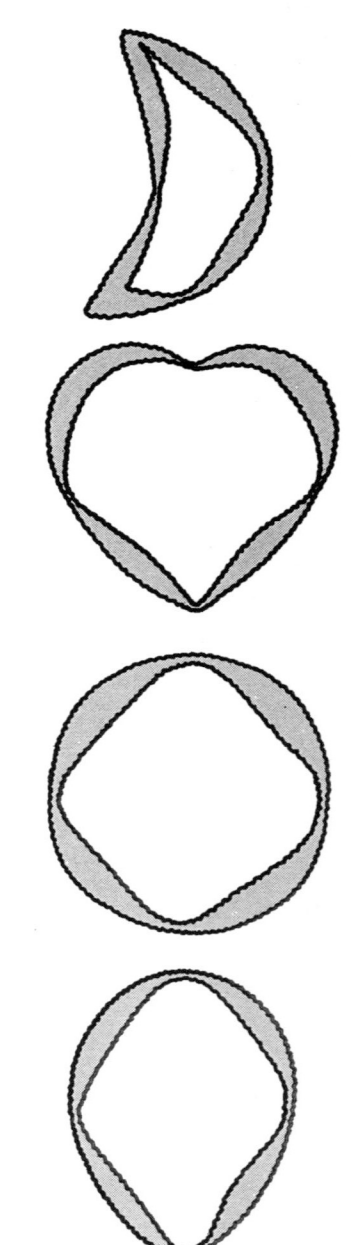

These shapes match.

2

1. Circle the stem that is longer.

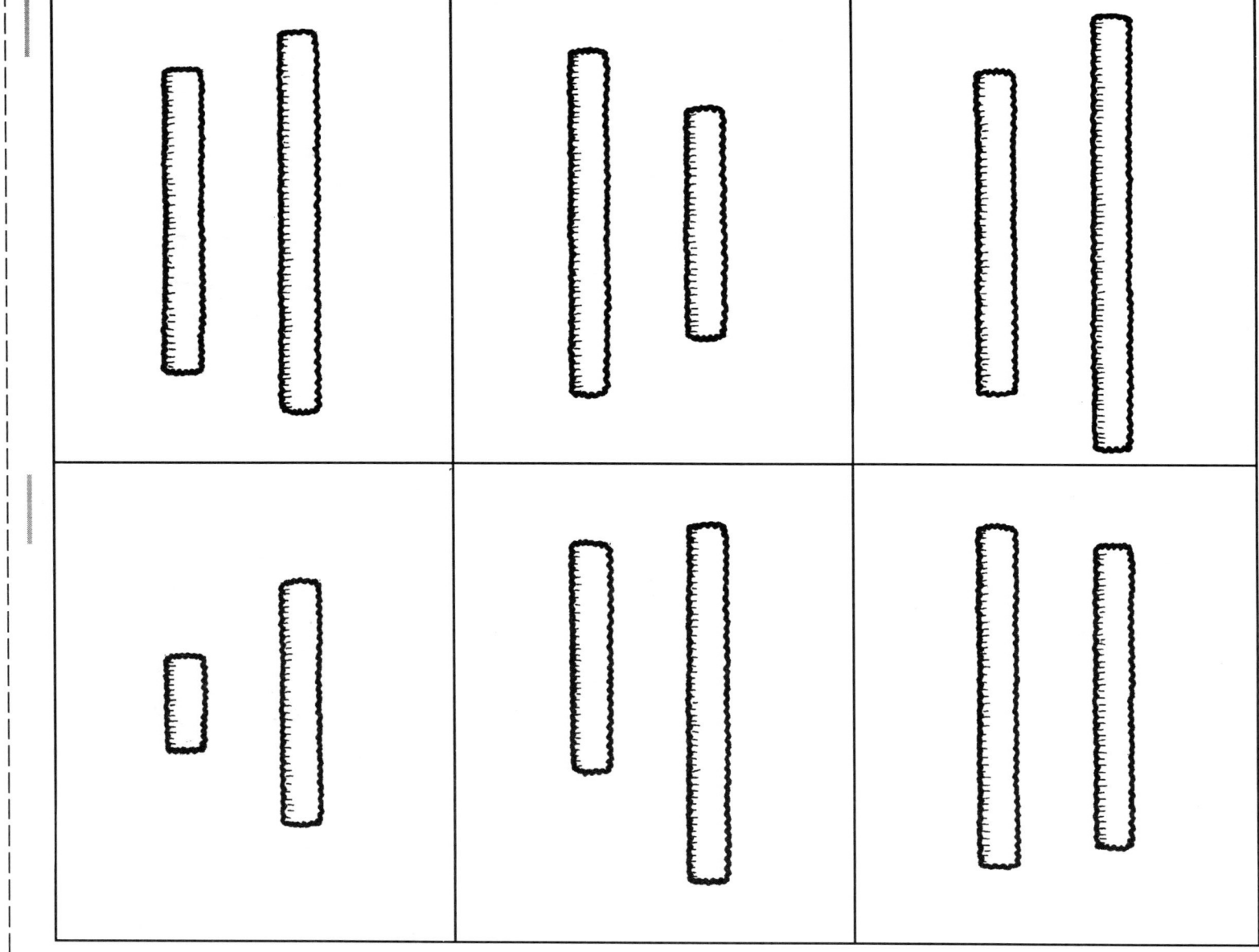

These stems are long.

1. How many stems are in each vase? Write the number in the box.

2. Draw flowers to match.

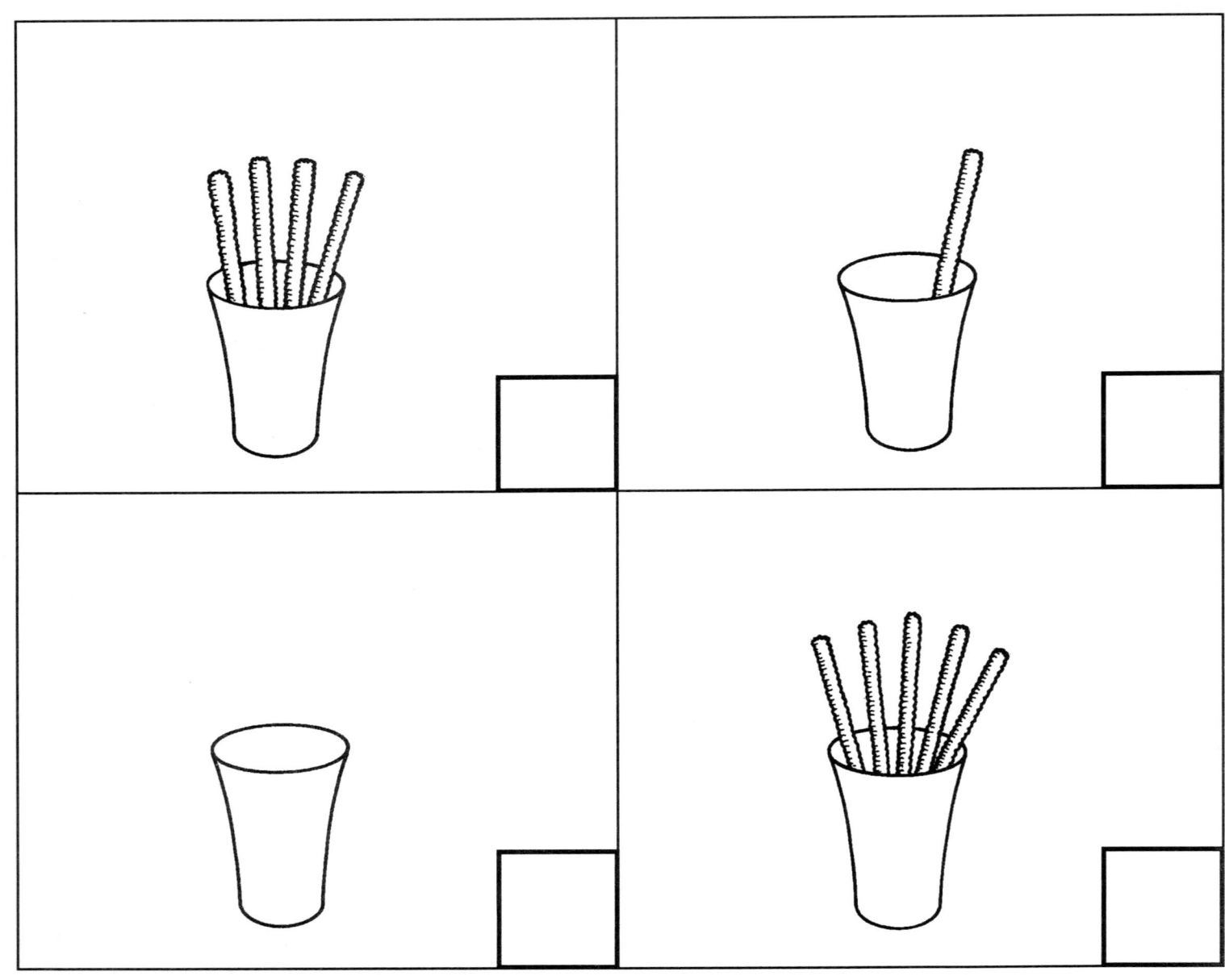

I can count stems.

4

1. Sing the song.
2. Color the picture.

Sung to: "Mary Had a Little Lamb"

We made things with the wire,
With the wire, with the wire.
We made things with the wire.
We had so much fun!

Totline Publications

Early Learning Resources
Songs, activities, themes, recipes, and tips

Celebrations
Easy, practical ideas for celebrating holidays and special days around the world. Plus ideas for making ordinary days special.
- **Celebrating Likes and Differences**
- **Small World Celebrations**
- **Special Day Celebrations**
- **Great Big Holiday Celebrations**

Theme-A-Saurus
Classroom-tested, around-the-curriculum activities organized into imaginative units. Great for implementing child-directed programs.
- **Multisensory Theme-A-Saurus**
- **Theme-A-Saurus**
- **Theme-A-Saurus II**
- **Toddler Theme-A-Saurus**
- **Alphabet Theme-A-Saurus**
- **Nursery Rhyme Theme-A-Saurus**
- **Storytime Theme-A-Saurus**

1•2•3 Series
Open-ended, age-appropriate, cooperative, and no-lose experiences for working with preschool children.
- **1•2•3 Art**
- **1•2•3 Games**
- **1•2•3 Colors**
- **1•2•3 Puppets**
- **1•2•3 Reading & Writing**
- **1•2•3 Rhymes, Stories & Songs**
- **1•2•3 Math**
- **1•2•3 Science**
- **1•2•3 Shapes**

Snacks Series
Easy, educational recipes for healthy eating and expanded learning.
- **Super Snacks**
- **Healthy Snacks**
- **Teaching Snacks**
- **Multicultural Snacks**

Piggyback Songs
New songs sung to the tunes of childhood favorites. No music to read! Easy for adults and children to learn. Chorded for guitar or autoharp.
- **Piggyback Songs**
- **More Piggyback Songs**
- **Piggyback Songs for Infants & Toddlers**
- **Piggyback Songs in Praise of God**
- **Piggyback Songs in Praise of Jesus**
- **Holiday Piggyback Songs**
- **Animal Piggyback Songs**
- **Piggyback Songs for School**
- **Piggyback Songs to Sign**
- **Spanish Piggyback Songs**
- **More Piggyback Songs for School**

Busy Bees
These seasonal books help two- and three-year-olds discover the world around them through their senses. Each book includes fun activity and learning ideas, songs, snack ideas, and more!
- **Busy Bees—SPRING**
- **Busy Bees—SUMMER**
- **Busy Bees—FALL**
- **Busy Bees—WINTER**

101 Tips for Directors
Great ideas for managing a preschool or daycare. These hassle-free, handy hints are a great help.
- **Staff and Parent Self-Esteem**
- **Parent Communication**
- **Health and Safety**
- **Marketing Your Center**
- **Resources for You and Your Center**
- **Child Development Training**

101 Tips for Toddler Teachers
Designed for adults who work with toddlers.
- **Classroom Management**
- **Discovery Play**
- **Dramatic Play**
- **Large Motor Play**
- **Small Motor Play**
- **Word Play**

101 Tips for Preschool Teachers
Valuable, fresh ideas for adults who work with young children.
- **Creating Theme Environments**
- **Encouraging Creativity**
- **Developing Motor Skills**
- **Developing Language Skills**
- **Teaching Basic Concepts**
- **Spicing Up Learning Centers**

Problem Solving Safari
Designed to help children problem-solve and think for themselves. Each book includes scenarios from children's real play and possible solutions.
- **Problem Solving Safari—Art**
- **Problem Solving Safari—Blocks**
- **Problem Solving Safari—Dramatic Play**
- **Problem Solving Safari—Manipulatives**
- **Problem Solving Safari—Outdoors**
- **Problem Solving Safari—Science**

The Best of Totline Series
Collections of some of the finest, most useful material published in *Totline Magazine* over the years.
- **The Best of Totline**
- **The Best of Totline Parent Flyers**

Totline Publications
Early Learning Resources
Posters, puzzles, and books for parents and children

A Year of Fun
Age-specific books detailing how young children grow and change and what parents can do to lay a foundation for later learning.
- Just for Babies
- Just for Ones
- Just for Twos
- Just for Threes
- Just for Fours
- Just for Fives

Getting Ready for School
Fun, easy-to-follow ideas for developing essential skills that preschoolers need before they can successfully achieve higher levels of learning.
- Ready to Learn Colors, Shapes, and Numbers
- Ready to Write and Develop Motor Skills
- Ready to Read
- Ready to Communicate
- Ready to Listen and Explore the Senses

Learning Everywhere
Everyday opportunities for teaching children about language, art, science, math, problem solving, self-esteem, and more!
- Teaching House
- Teaching Town
- Teaching Trips

Beginning Fun With Art
Introduce young children to the fun of art while developing coordination skills and building self-confidence.
- Craft Sticks • Crayons • Felt
- Glue • Paint • Paper Shapes
- Modeling Dough • Yarn
- Tissue Paper • Scissors
- Rubber Stamps • Stickers

Beginning Fun With Science
Make science fun with these quick, safe, easy-to-do activities that lead to discovery and spark the imagination.
- Bugs & Butterflies
- Plants & Flowers
- Magnets
- Rainbows & Colors
- Sand & Shells
- Water & Bubbles

Teaching Tales
Each of these children's books includes a delightful story plus related activity ideas that expand on the story's theme.
- Kids Celebrate the Alphabet
- Kids Celebrate Numbers

Seeds for Success™
For parents who want to plant the seeds for success in their young children
- Growing Creative Kids
- Growing Happy Kids
- Growing Responsible Kids
- Growing Thinking Kids

Learn With Piggyback® Songs
BOOKS AND TAPES
Age-appropriate songs that help children learn!
- Songs & Games for Babies
- Songs & Games for Toddlers
- Songs & Games for Threes
- Songs & Games for Fours

Learning Puzzles
Designed to challenge as children grow.
- Kids Celebrate Numbers
- Kids Celebrate the Alphabet
- Bear Hugs 4-in-1 Puzzle Set
- Busy Bees 4-in-1 Puzzle Set

Two-Sided Circle Puzzles
Double-sided, giant floor puzzles designed in a circle with cutout pieces for extra learning and fun.
- Underwater Adventure
- African Adventure

We Work & Play Together Posters
A colorful collection of cuddly bear posters showing adult and children bears playing and working together.
- We Build Together
- We Cook Together
- We Play Together
- We Read Together
- We Sing Together
- We Work Together

Bear Hugs® Health Posters
Encourage young children to develop good health habits. Additional learning activities on back!
- We Brush Our Teeth
- We Can Exercise
- We Cover our Coughs and Sneezes
- We Eat Good Food
- We Get Our Rest
- We Wash Our Hands

Reminder Posters
Photographic examples of children following the rules.
- I cover my coughs
- I listen quietly
- I pick up my toys
- I put my things away
- I say please and thank you
- I share
- I use words when I am angry
- I wash my hands
- I wipe my nose

Totline products are available at fine parent and teacher stores. For the dealer nearest you, call 1-800-421-5565.

If you like Totline® Books, you'll love Totline® Magazine!

For fresh ideas that challenge and engage young children in active learning, reach for **Totline Magazine**—Proven ideas from innovative teachers!

Each issue includes

- Seasonal learning themes
- Stories, songs, and rhymes
- Open-ended art projects
- Science explorations
- Reproducible parent pages
- Ready-made teaching materials
- Activities just for toddlers
- Reproducible healthy snack recipes
- Special pull-outs

Receive a free copy of Totline® Magazine by calling 800-609-1724 for subscription information.